30 POWERFUL STORIES AND LESSONS
ABOUT LEADERSHIP, LIFE, AND LOVE
FROM MY DEAF PARENTS

MOM DAD NOT HEAR

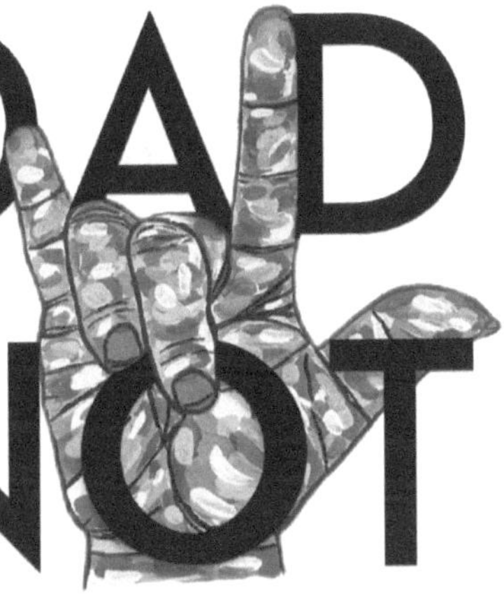

MICKEY CAROLAN

WITH KATHLEEN & JOSEPH SINDORF

Third Culture Books
An imprint of Third Culture Books LLC
Byron Center, Michigan

Most Third Culture Books are available at a discount when purchased in large quantities. For more information, please email mickey@mickeycarolan.com.

Published by Third Culture Books.
Written with Kathleen & Joseph Sindorf
Editing by Phil deHaan
Cover Artwork by Diana Lopez
Cover and Interior Book Design by Miblart
Author Photograph by Michelle Cuppy

ISBN: 979-8-9879923-6-4 (Hardcover)
ISBN: 979-8-9879923-7-1 (Paperback)
ISBN: 979-8-9879923-8-8 (eBook)

Library of Congress Control Number: 2023919432

Printed in the United States of America

MOM DAD NOT HEAR

"A must-read for those building cultures of Belonging. Carolan takes readers on an identity journey filled with authenticity and purpose to unite us all." - **Kim Dabbs, Author of You Belong Here**

"Anyone who grows up in a challenging situation will often see their condition as a burden. It isn't until later in life that you realize you were given a gift. In this book, Mickey provides a lot of great stories and wisdom from his experience as a CODA (which is my childhood experience as well). Best of all, he tells the overarching story that challenges in your life can either crush you or strengthen you ... and that it's up to you how you want to interpret those circumstances." - **Bill McKendry, author of DO MORE GOOD : Moving nonprofits from good to growth and one of the key people who helped launch the He Gets Us movement, the largest Jesus campaign in history.**

"Mom Dad Not Hear is heartfelt and valuable for readers of all ages. It shares impactful stories that helped mold and create passionate leadership strategies within the author, Mickey Carolan. Readers will fall in love with the life lessons learned and the extraordinary life of a CODA. This book is a must-read!" - **Lane Walker, Award-Winning and Best-Selling Author**

"An enlightening journey through the eyes of a child with Deaf parents, this book beautifully demonstrates the unique life and communication lessons from such an upbringing. It also offers insightful applications of these lessons in broader aspects of life for everyone." - **Alexis Ander Kashar, Civil Rights Attorney and Entrepreneur**

"Not only is Mom Dad Not Hear an inspiring personal narrative, but it also serves as a reminder of the beauty of our unique, diverse backgrounds. Woven with poignant lessons, this book provides readers an opportunity to learn, self-reflect, and grow. 'Finish' was Mickey's word of the year for 2023; I disagree... he's only getting started." - **Sue Schmidlkofer, UPS Diversity, Equity & Inclusion**

"As a fellow CODA, I've never related to a book so much in my life - a mix of hilarity, heartfelt moments, and wonderful life lessons. This is a book that will stay with you long after you've closed the final chapter." – **Brad Klein, The CODA Comedian**

"Mom Dad Not Hear captivates readers across diverse cultures through relatable family narratives. Its profound leadership insights elevate it beyond any other book addressing the experiences of having Deaf parents that I've encountered." – **Keith Wann - CODA, Entertainer, and Interpreter**

"I have come to greatly respect his business acumen, big-picture vision, and straight-shooter approach to the work we do. So, it was no surprise when I read his most recent book and found it filled with wonderful insights that weave together his life as a CODA with his life as a husband, father, and business leader. His book is one I will return to repeatedly, and I know its deep wisdom will stand the test of time." - **Deb Atwood, Executive Director of Deaf and Hard of Hearing Services**

"This book is a great read! The stories are so interesting and provide a real insight into understanding what it's like to be a CODA. At the same time, you are learning new management communication skills. It's a win-win read!" - **Cheri Dowling, Executive Director of the American Society for Deaf Children**

Dedication

To family... past, present, and future. This book is dedicated to the enduring legacies that flow through our veins, connecting us to our roots and propelling us toward the unknown. Together, let us honor our shared stories and leave behind a reminder of love, wisdom, and boundless possibility.

TABLE OF CONTENTS

AUTHOR'S NOTE

d/Deaf Disclaimer

I'll admit it, I am sensitive about how d/Deaf people want to identify themselves.

If you picked up this book and are not familiar with the topic, you may initially be thrown off by seeing the word "Deaf" being capitalized in the middle of a sentence. It isn't a mistake. It's intentional. The community I was raised in almost always capitalized the D.

There are three main labels or descriptives used when referring to people who cannot hear: Deaf with an uppercase D, deaf with a lowercase d, and "hard of hearing." The capitalized term "Deaf" is used to identify the unique group of people who cannot hear who share common characteristics such as language, culture, and community. The word "deaf" (written without capitalization) is only used when referring to the physical condition of total or major hearing loss. And the term "hard of hearing" is used to describe those who have a lesser degree of hearing loss.

Capitalizing the word Deaf recognizes the status of this group in much the same way that other commonly used group names like African American, Jewish, and Hispanic are capitalized.

Throughout this book, I've been extremely diligent in making sure d/Deaf is used as correctly as possible. This detail is important to me because the Deaf community where I was raised has been very significant to me. But I am human, and I probably made a mistake or two somewhere on these pages. Please know that if you find an error, it was not intentional. I apologize, and I hope you hear in my words the love and honor I have for that wonderful group of people who are Deaf.

~Mickey

INTRODUCTION

If not now, when?

That question is what I asked myself at the beginning of this year. I realized that our children were growing older, and as a family, we were on the cusp of getting busier and busier with extracurricular activities. I knew that time was about to be an ever more precious commodity.

Since I couldn't answer that question with any certainty of a clear future date, I knew the answer had to be *now*! So, I jumped in. I've always wanted to be an author. In fact, I still have my elementary school "Young Author" t-shirt to prove it.

This book didn't burst into being this year. Its bones were created as part of National Novel Writing Month (NaNoWriMo) in 2014. In that challenge, you write 50,000 words in thirty days. I completed it, even though most of those 50,000 words sucked. I'm a much better writer now than I was in 2014.

Why?

When I told people I was writing a book, the first question I often got was, "Why?" The honest answer is that it was a voice within me I couldn't silence...a desire that burned like a fire in me...it was something I knew I had to do. The rest of the answer centers around generational history and legacy. I'm in the middle of it now. I couldn't answer detailed questions about my family history beyond my great-grandparents if I were asked.

This book is equal parts memoir, education, and advice. There is only one category this book fits into perfectly, and that category is real. This book is real.

Let me take you on a journey as I share stories and lessons from my forty-plus years of living as a CODA (Child of Deaf Adults) and the incredible impact my Deaf parents have had on me.

3 & 30

Three Parts. Thirty lessons. One for each day in a month.

As you turn these pages, I intend to share with you thirty stories and lessons that will educate and provide perspective about the Deaf community. It will not read like a traditional memoir. That is on purpose.

I have read many written works by fellow CODA authors. Many were good, some were great, but none have been structured like this book.

If you love reading leadership books, I've got you covered.

If you love reading stories about life, again, I've got you covered.

If you love reading love stories, you guessed it, you're covered.

So, if nothing else, you are about to read a book that is different!

Whether you smile, laugh, or cry as you read this book, I hope that it positively impacts your life.

Let's go!

Mom Dad Not Hear

PART ONE

LEADERSHIP

Mom Dad Not Hear

MOM, DAD NOT HEAR

*"Pretend those around you are deaf to your words.
Let your actions speak and communicate your feelings
and intentions. This way of living ensures the potency
of your message is delivered and serves as a gauge
against our verbal nonsense."*
Dr. Steve Maraboli, author and speaker

1985

The phone rings. The sound comes from an old, faded-yellow, rotary-dial, landline telephone attached to the wall in our kitchen. I look up, slide off the couch, shuffle over to the phone, and answer it. Just like every other time it rings—because I know nobody else in the house is going to do it.

"Hello?" I answer with a small, questioning, childish voice.

There was a brief silence, and then a man's voice on the other end of the line stammers, looking for the right words, "Uh...hello...well...can I speak with Mr. Car-o-lan?"

"Um..." Another quiet response from me: "Mom, Dad not hear."

"Excuse me, what did you say?" asks the incredulous man on the other end of the phone, obviously trying to comprehend my answer.

"Mom, Dad not hear," I repeat.

I hear an exasperated gasp and then *click*, the call disconnects, and the man's voice is replaced by the low hum of a dial tone. I shake my head, staring at the phone handset, wondering what's going on.

Fifteen minutes later, as I'm back on the couch, I hear a strong knock at the front door of our house. I wave at my father and point at the door (that's my way of telling him someone is at the door). He raises his 5-foot-11-inch, 220-pound frame out of his favorite chair and makes his way to the door. He opens it and sees two stern police officers—sent to our house because of a child welfare concern.

The police officers notice a puzzled look on my father's face, and they ask if there is a child in the house. My father becomes anxious and taps his finger on his right ear multiple times trying to get the two policemen to understand that he is Deaf. As he continues to tap his ear, he makes vocal sounds, using his mostly unintelligible audible tones, trying to communicate that he can't hear what they are saying. His frustrated attempts fail.

When he realizes that the officers have not understood what he's trying to express, he holds up one finger as if to say, "Wait one second." He goes to the telephone, dials my grandmother's number, and hands the receiver to the officer. My grandmother and the officer have a quick discussion during which she verifies that there is indeed a child residing at that house with his parents—who are Deaf, or as the boy said, they "not hear." But, besides that, all is well at the home. The officers shake my dad's hand and leave to go about their business.

That was the moment when I realized that clear communication takes real effort, and that it is everyone's responsibility. And I was only four years old.

The best leaders communicate clearly

Now, nearly four decades later, I grasp the importance of that early lesson. I have witnessed it firsthand in my professional career. I have been with the same market-leading international organization for more than twenty years and held eleven leadership positions across four different departments, and the story has been the same in every single role. Clear communication takes real effort, and it is everyone's responsibility.

But just because we all share the responsibility doesn't mean that it works all the time! Some people don't expect it to take effort. They don't invest the time needed to truly understand others and clarify their messages. That's when miscommunication happens—sometimes over something as simple as homophones, words that sound the same but can have very different meanings...like "hear" and "here."

And as I found out at four years of age, a simple breakdown of communication can bring the police to your front door.

One thing I've consistently witnessed in my career is a direct correlation between the best leaders and their skill at communicating clearly. And it's not just skill—it takes persistence. They keep at it, don't give up until they are understood, and understand the messages coming back to them. These leaders often have different styles and personalities, and they communicate in different ways, but they have this in common: they value clear communication, and they know how to deliver a message to their teams with 100 percent clarity.

In the Deaf community, we often use the term, "Deaf blunt" to describe how direct and abbreviated communication can be among non-hearing people. When a person is Deaf blunt, they will tell you how they think, what they want, and how they feel—without pulling any punches or beating around the bush. The interaction can be so direct that many hearing people would think it rude. It's the equivalent of using American Sign Language—precise and to the point, without using any unnecessary words.

Most leaders operate in the hearing world, which can be good and bad for the effectiveness of a leader's communication. On the one hand, a leader in the hearing world has a much easier time providing context to a message they are trying to relay. They can try to soften the message and make it more palatable to their listener. But that can also be a detriment since too much context can dilute the real intended objective of the message.

My leadership communication style slides on a scale between Deaf blunt and contextual, because of my exposure to the nuances in communication within both the Deaf and hearing worlds. On one side of the scale is my ability to communicate directly when needed. On the other side of the scale, I can add context to the situation and messaging, if it's called for. Every time I communicate with someone, I work hard to ensure that my messaging is delivered at the right place on that scale.

Leadership is not a one-size-fits-all proposition, and the best leaders are those who can flex and adapt to provide what will make a difference. If you can accurately diagnose a situation and then pivot to meet the needs at that time, you will be successful. The best leaders I've observed are sensitive to the people they are communicating with. They think about the hearer's needs and state of mind, so they can vary their communication style to fit their listener's mood and personality. Good leadership doesn't mean insisting on using one style of communication that never changes, but it is flexible and adaptable, thinking more about the other person than you do about yourself.

Today, try using a sliding scale of communication—based on your recipient's needs—rather than your own state of mind. Listen with your eyes as well as your ears to understand the best way to talk to people on your team. And watch out for those homophones. They can really confuse a listener!

THE DEAF MENU

"Every one of us is blind and deaf until
our eyes are opened to our fellowmen, until
our ears hear the voice of humanity."
Helen Keller, blind and deaf author, advocate, and activist

I got you a different menu

My mother and father always found a way for us to eat like royalty while our family was on vacation. We didn't darken the door of the true high-end steak houses, but we ate well and definitely at a higher level than we were used to at home. Back then, going to almost any restaurant was what we considered to be fancy dining.

We're enjoying a family trip to Florida, and my parents see the sign for a familiar restaurant, a chain that they love. As expected, we enter the restaurant, and the hostess seats our party, and gives each of us a menu. As we're deciding between ribs, chicken tenders, or something else, the waitress begins taking our drink order. The server starts with my mother and asks what she'd like to drink. I jump in and start to speak for her, and suddenly the waitress gets a panicked look on her face. All frustrated, she pulls the menus out of my parents' hands, hurries back toward the kitchen, and disappears out of sight.

Mom signs to me, "Why? What happened?"

Dad signs, "BS!"

The waitress returns, beaming from ear to ear—obviously proud of herself. She hands new menus to my parents, while slowly and clearly declaring, "I got you a different menu!"

Dad holds up the new menu and signs to me, "What's this?"

Mom signs back, "She thinks blind."

Yes, the new menus were in Braille!

I'm laughing so hard internally, but somehow, I manage to keep my composure. I turn to the waitress and explain, "Miss, my parents are Deaf, not blind." Once again, she gets flustered, grabs the Braille menus, dashes off, and sheepishly returns with the original menus.

I guess one "handicapped menu" is expected to cover all potential customers who come in with special needs!

Intentions only go so far

My father often reminded me that being Deaf doesn't make you dumb, but it sure can make those around you seem dumb and dumber. My mother would often add that their intentions may be good, but their actions are misplaced.

This restaurant story is just one humorous reminder of an ongoing set of scenarios I've encountered growing up, where people would make poor decisions, even though they probably had good intentions. In most situations, I'm certain that the intentions of the people interacting with my parents were good. But because of how they executed their actions, their good intentions were watered down to a point where they weren't recognized by my parents as anything but ignorance, and sometimes it caused a tense situation. At times, such unwarranted actions drew attention to my parents' differences and embarrassed all of us.

This is why you often hear, "Great leaders lead by example." That phrase is action-based. Great leaders understand that it is not enough to have good intentions. They know their intentions, coupled with appropriate actions, are what it takes to bring excellent results.

Leaders can benefit from this reminder when talking with their team members. Great leaders will be intentional in their communication and then swiftly act upon the follow-up items they discussed. When following that model, the intentionality and the follow-up constitute the leader's effective actions.

When you lead by example, you don't just encourage and push your team members to pursue excellence—rather, you actively demonstrate on a daily and moment-by-moment basis what excellence looks like. You lead from the front, rather than from the sidelines or the back of the pack. Leading by example is the difference between saying, "You can do this" and instead saying, "We can do this together," or "Let me show you what works for me." Though the first statement shows support and encouragement, the second statement builds connection, camaraderie, and trust, and the third statement gives the team the confidence that they know what you want and that you can teach it by example. You know what you're talking about.

People who lead by example are actively demonstrating that they value their team's work by carrying some of the weight themselves. Leading by example can increase your team engagement. Remember that the people you manage are watching you and learning from how you react to challenges! If what you're doing and saying is inconsistent, that inconsistency can lead to frustration and a lack of trust. But if you can model the right, consistent example to your team, you'll inspire them to follow and give their best effort, too.

Today, think about how you can lead by example as an authentic leader. Show your team more than your good intentions. Model for them the values and behaviors you are hoping to see in them—and nurture them as they grow!

HOW TO GET A DEAF PERSON'S ATTENTION

*"And the blind man said to the deaf man,
'Do you see what I hear?'"*
Wayne Gerard Trotman, author and playwright

It's a different ballgame

"Hey Elloree, can you grab my notebook from upstairs please?" As I sit here in my office, writing and drinking coffee loaded with hazelnut creamer on a Saturday morning, it's simple to get someone's attention in a hearing household. If you yell loud enough, someone will hear you!

Now, let's play out that same scenario in a Deaf household. In this setting, there are three options. One: I could get up and get the notebook myself. Two: I could grab a soft object and throw it outside of my office in hopes that someone might see it and come ask me what I wanted. Three: I could get up and flash the light in the room repeatedly, again in hopes that someone would see the flashing light and come ask me what I need. Here is a hint: Option One is the obvious choice if you want something to get done quickly.

Another example is when I would come home from college for a weekend. I would usually arrive late on a Friday night, after dark. My parents' home was in a small town where they felt comfortable leaving the door unlocked. Most kids walk into their home and say, "Mom, Dad, I'm home." My version of that in a house with two Deaf parents was walking into the house and flicking the kitchen light on and off repeatedly so that they could see it from the living room and know I was home. Otherwise, they might jump up startled when I suddenly appeared in the room!

Ways CODAs get their parents' attention...

- Tap on their shoulder
- Wave their hands
- Flash the lights on and off
- Stomp on the floor
- Bang on the table
- Throw soft objects into the room where they are

It would be great if we could read minds and know when somebody in the next room wants something so we wouldn't have to flash lights or throw things. Unfortunately, most of us don't have that kind of extra-sensory perception. We need to use what we have at hand. One of those things was a stash of small soft footballs that sat next to the recliner in the living room. Years of throwing the footballs gave me a heightened ability to predict how the conversation would go based on their reaction to the football being thrown at them.

The best leaders have situational awareness

Many people are familiar with Michel de Nostredame, whose name has been Latinized as Nostradamus. He became famous for predicting many major world events.

Throughout my career, I have predicted major events, both internally and externally. I have had numerous conversations with colleagues and friends where they told me my predictions were correct. I was often called a "little Nostradamus."

I attribute much of my predictive ability to being raised as a CODA. Growing up with Deaf parents forces you to become more observant and intuitive. I needed to be constantly alert to their unspoken needs and quick to pick up whatever signals they might use: a flash of room lights, waving hands, or something landing on the floor a few feet from me... that meant Mom or Dad needed something!

The best leaders pay attention to all the signals around them—sometimes it's called situational awareness. They use the input that they take in to help them make educated decisions and adjust quickly. Gifted, decisive leaders move rapidly from observation to action. That speed allows them to create a solution before most people have even realized there is a problem.

Being able to look for clues and subtle changes takes practiced observation skills and keen mindfulness. Paying attention to your surroundings enables you, as a leader, to make adjustments to your team before your peers. You can also hedge towards changing tactics that will allow your team to keep winning against your competitors and navigate the global environment in a much more agile fashion.

Today, work at observing the signals around you. Pay attention to the numbers and metrics that you use to measure growth and be quick to react before a slight dip becomes a trend. Watch your team—ensuring that they are at peak performance and mutually benefiting the whole. View what goes on around you today, both with a critical eye and with a vision pointed toward the future. Retain what you see and use that raw data to create a better tomorrow for your team, your family, and you!

DRIVER'S TRAINING

"Straight roads do not make skillful drivers."
Paulo Coelho de Souza, author

Riding shotgun

Think back to when you first learned how to drive. Likely, one of your parents rode shotgun when you had your learner's permit and practiced your skills. Your hands gripped the wheel at 10 and 2, your eyes were forward, scanning from ditch to ditch, and you were very focused. You wanted to log the required hours so you could get that coveted driver's license.

At some point during your drive, your adult passenger might have said, "Turn right at the next intersection." Easy, peasy and that's exactly how my practice drives went with our class instructors. When my classmates did their driving practice, their primary distraction was deciding which parent would go driving with them. Was it the laid-back one or the uptight one?

Driving with my parents was quite different from what I experienced driving with my instructors or what my classmates encountered with their parents. Like most families, mine had one laid-back co-pilot, my father, and a more uptight one, my mother. She still denies being uptight to this day, but my memory says otherwise.

Driving with a Deaf co-pilot was very different. I could turn the radio on. That never would happen with my official driving instructor. I also would receive no verbal commands during the drive, unless, of course, I was about to put the car in the ditch. Then that wasn't so much a verbal command, it was more of a yell of horror! Both my parents understood that trying to use verbal commands would not be very clear and could even be startling to me. If I was going too fast, I'd see a flat hand, palm facing down, moving up and down. Navigation directions were given using the "L" sign to tell me to turn left, the "R" sign to turn right, and they would use a flat hand turned sideways and moving forward to indicate that they wanted me to go straight.

My younger sister and only sibling, observed my experiences of practice driving with our parents and realized that she could arrange her schedule to do most of her hours of driving after dark, resulting in a significant reduction in hand signals and corrective ASL signs. It was a brilliant move that reduced the stress of learning to drive for her.

Do not let the noises be a distraction

The first thing many of us do when we get in the car is turn on the radio. One thing I learned from observing my parents' driving is that you are much less distracted when one of your five senses is not being used for a different task. Admittedly, even though I learned that lesson during driver education and know it is valid, I still choose to drive with the radio on. I believe I have learned how to keep the noise of the radio from being a distraction while I'm driving.

"Noise" isn't only produced by the radio. It is also a distraction that can come from a variety of sources and force itself into our daily lives and careers. Possible distractions could be your sales projections coming out late, promotional rhetoric from competitors, and of course, the constant distracting noise emanating from the rumor mill. In our personal lives, political discourse and social media posts are full of noise that can distract us and make us less productive.

When I am faced with noise that attempts to steal my attention, I assert control and instruct my mind to judge it against the core objectives I've set for my life. If the noise doesn't contribute to a positive impact on my core objectives, I do not allow it to get more of my attention.

Now, here is the tricky part—if you're the leader of a team, how do you help your team members do a course correction when they get distracted? It will happen eventually in every team. One successful strategy I've found is using questions to check their distraction level. First, I check their mental health, with empathy, and then, throughout the short conversation, I use questions to bring them back to center. I may not eliminate all the noise and distractions in their lives, but as a leader, it is my job to try with all my might to keep them on course.

A focused team that's not distracted is a productive team.

You can control your thoughts and your actions. Part of that control is not allowing the noise around you to become a distraction and steal your attention and your productivity. Start today—take control of your thought life. Ask yourself if each hobby, interest, and activity is contributing positively to your life goals. If not, turn the volume down or turn it off!

HEAVY ARE THE HANDS THAT FORM THE SIGNS

"Uneasy lies the head that wears a crown."
William Shakespeare, playwright

Even important things get tiresome

I'm only twelve years old and about to negotiate the purchase of a vehicle, a gold-colored Chevrolet Astro van. It obviously isn't for me as I wouldn't be able to legally drive a car for a few more years. No, this car is for my father.

As we're about to enter the dealership, my father stops, looks me in the eye, and signs, "I'm the boss." The meaning isn't lost on me. I have one job: to interpret for him. He is the customer and the negotiator. I'm just the middleman. (or maybe, since I'm twelve, the middleboy).

He needs me to understand my role because I've gradually gotten bored doing precise interpretation, and he knows it. Although, it's not so much that it is boring as it is difficult. It's just too much like work. I nod that I get it, and we walk into the showroom.

My father is a big man and an imposing figure. His idea of negotiation is to state a price, be firm, and never back down. That can work if those tough statements are said by a big imposing man. They don't work as well if they are spoken by the faltering pubescent voice of a twelve-year-old boy.

My presence did not match up with his demeanor. Even though the car salesman knows that my father is the customer, I'm the one doing the talking. Car salesmen are known for being fierce negotiators, and young boys are not. It's no surprise that we end up paying way too much for that car.

Responsibility is a weighty thing

In the quote by Shakespeare at the beginning of this chapter, King Henry IV laments, "Uneasy lies the head that wears a crown." He is complaining about his inability to sleep. Even in the calm middle of the night, with all the comfort he has around him, he is denied that. The soliloquy tells us that those who have no cares can sleep peacefully, but a king has great responsibilities that keep him awake at night.

Shakespeare's quote above is often misquoted as "Heavy is the head that wears the crown." As the oldest CODA in my family, I rephrase it as "Heavy are the hands that form the signs." When you're the first-born son of Deaf parents, it isn't a crown that weighs heavy with the responsibilities as the head of state, it's the signing that weighs you down with the responsibility of communicating clearly and well for your parents.

How old were you when you started scheduling your own medical appointments? How old were you when you called the bank to discuss your finances? I was five years old when I had the weight of making those calls for my parents.

The burden didn't stop with the need for me to interpret in difficult situations in which I was boxing way above my weight class, or swimming in water way over my head. I also felt the responsibility to determine when and where I would need to switch roles. Like many CODAs, I grew up having to be a chameleon. One minute I was a kid enjoying my friends, and the next minute I would be the interpreter between my parents and their hearing friends. Whenever I was out somewhere with my parents and another adult came up to us, I would immediately have to shed my kid skin and transform into functioning in my adult skin.

That burden of being a chameleon was sometimes heavier than having to stay poised in difficult adult conversations. Trying to navigate when and where to switch roles in the parent/child/interpreter dynamic was stressful.

Burdens can either crush you beneath their weight or they can strengthen you and impact you for good.

Be a chameleon

As I mentioned, I have held eleven leadership positions across four different departments, and I believe a key reason I have had success in multiple positions and departments is that I learned at an early age how to be a chameleon. I had a childhood of versatility, so I had to learn to adapt quickly. At any given moment, I could transition to any role.

Every time I changed roles within my company—and particularly when I changed departments—there was stress, resulting from my being initially stretched out of my comfort zone. But in comparison with my transitions as a kid, those corporate position moves were painless. I was an adult dealing with adults. I was no longer a twelve-year-old boy who felt the burden of constantly switching roles and navigating complex social and business situations.

I know some readers are shaking their heads right now. They would say that being a chameleon is akin to being a fake—that you should know who you are and be the best version of that person that you can be.

That reminds me of a question that has been debated throughout time...should you become an expert at one particular thing or become very good at multiple things? I've decided that it's up to each of us individually to determine which option best suits our interests, goals, and lifestyles. My many roles and responsibilities as a CODA required that

I develop a broad skill set and become very good at all of my roles, so I know which side I stand on when it comes to this debate.

While I have had to be a chameleon since an early age, I've still carried the same high level of character and integrity from role to role. I never thought there was any other way. I hold a high standard for my character, in large part because every single role I had to take on when I was younger required an elevated degree of ethics and responsibility.

Being a chameleon doesn't mean you are indecisive, deceptive, or easily influenced. It is quite the opposite. To be a chameleon, you must be well-rounded, possess varied experience, and be adaptable to changing situations and environments. In the wild, chameleons escape the attention of predators because they completely adapt to their surroundings. That keeps them from being attacked and allows them to quietly acquire what they need to thrive in every changing environment. Likewise, business leaders who have chameleon traits welcome change and blend in with the chaos and crisis situations that sometimes surround them, navigating the path to success for their employees.

You will invariably face role changes in some capacity in your lifetime, and I encourage you to be a chameleon. Be flexible! Today, start by embracing and strengthening your multiple skills and abilities. As you become a versatile leader, establish your high character, practice blending in when you enter the zone of discomfort, and become proficient at adapting to the changes life and work will throw at you.

Chameleons change their appearance as a means of protection and stealth. That same skill has helped sustain me in every role throughout my life. I suggest you give it a try starting today!

ON THE BRINK OF CLOSING

*"Enough is enough. We need a comprehensive,
full-service agency addressing the needs of our
Deaf and Hard of Hearing communities."*
Marty & Dianne Jansen, founders, Deaf and Hard
of Hearing Services

Deaf and Hard of Hearing Services

"I'm writing personal checks to pay the employees and haven't taken a paycheck myself in months." I can't believe what I'm hearing as I listen to the executive director of Deaf and Hard of Hearing Services talk openly to the organization's board of directors.

I am a guest at this board meeting. Earlier, I heard the story of how this organization was founded, and I was moved to seek them out and get involved.

The story goes something like this...

One late night in 1995, Marty Jansen, a Deaf community leader, woke up suddenly from a sound sleep, clutching his chest. He was having a heart attack. His wife Dianne was awakened by the commotion. She realized the seriousness of the moment and rushed to the phone. Dianne was severely hard of hearing, so she called 911 using a TTY (a telecommunications device for the Deaf), but the 911 operator kept disconnecting the call. In desperation, Dianne finally decided to use the normal phone to call 911. Although she couldn't hear any response, she used her voice to repeatedly tell the operator their address and request an ambulance.

It worked. Fortunately, Dianne had just enough intelligible speech to communicate the urgency of the message and get a timely response. If she wasn't there, and Marty was on his own, he would have died. Like most Deaf people, Marty's ability to speak and be understood was almost nonexistent.

Upon their arrival at the hospital, the medical personnel called a well-known interpreter, and she was able to rush over to the emergency room and provide interpretation services for the couple and the medical team. However, because the hospital did not have a roster of interpreters for the Deaf, the interpreter was stuck interpreting for hours on end. When the interpreter finally had to leave, the Jansens were left wondering when they would get the next interpreter, if ever. And indeed, the endless search for adequate interpreting services continued throughout their entire stay in the hospital. Dianne struggled to hear what the doctors were asking, often having no option but to interpret the best she could for her husband. They were extremely fortunate that there were no serious miscommunications that impacted Marty's treatment. Others have not been so lucky.

When word spread of their emergency and the difficulty accessing qualified interpretation services, it was the final straw for many people. Interpreters, hearing service providers, and those who were Deaf and hard of hearing themselves, including the Jansens, came together and said, "Enough is enough. We need a comprehensive, full-service agency addressing the needs of our Deaf and Hard of Hearing communities."

That's how Deaf and Hard of Hearing Services was born. Today, D&HHS has become what it was originally envisioned to be: a comprehensive, full-service agency serving the needs of the Deaf, Deaf/Blind, and Hard of Hearing communities. To this day, D&HHS remains the only agency in West Michigan providing comprehensive services to this population. Yet so much work remains to be done.[1]

As I sat in that board meeting, listening to the executive director's dismal financial report, it was extremely clear that this vital agency was on the brink of bankruptcy and needed immediate help. Everyone around the table in that room had enormous hearts. But big hearts and great intentions won't pay the bills unless they are accompanied by a successful business model.

I knew something about successful business models. I had invested my entire career working for a company that never had a shortage of cash. Although I was just a guest in the meeting, I commented to the board that the agency was not treating itself as a business. There was no clear direction to grow top-line revenue and no clarity on the actions they should take to control costs. They all saw the need for someone to challenge them and help them to think differently about their financial situation. Needless to say, they elected a new member of their board of directors—me, the talkative guest.

With the leadership of the executive director and my recommendations, the agency got rid of their major capital liability, their office building. The mortgage on this old, dilapidated building couldn't be justified. Once the agency got out from underneath that monthly burden, they were able to focus on improving their top-line revenue number.

It was clear that revenues were driven by interpreter services. When the use of our interpreter services grew, our revenues also grew. So, we focused on forming and strengthening collaborative partnerships with businesses, schools, and hospital networks. Then, we sought out the best interpreters in the region and recruited them to work through our agency.

This wasn't a quick process. The first year, it was a battle just to break even. In year two, we revamped how we priced our interpretation services, bringing them in line with current expectations. In year three, we enhanced the back-end processes we used to fill interpreter jobs. In year four, 2019, the agency was finally in the best financial health it had ever been in. This process involved much hard work, along with several staff and board member changes, as the entire team was challenged to not only think with their hearts but also with their heads, as well.

Today, I am still part of the Board of Directors of this fine organization. I have seen its evolution from a very socially conscious board to a well-balanced board. When I first joined the board, the agency was a step away from turning off the lights and going out of business, and it didn't turn the tide until the board and the staff embraced a business mindset.

Get a business mindset

Deaf and Hard of Hearing Services' new offices are in the Special Olympics of Michigan facility as a result of a $250,000 capital campaign. Orchestrating that successful campaign was the cherry on top of my tenure as the board treasurer for D&HHS. After that, I passed the reins to another qualified board member.

This story highlights the importance of having a business mindset, especially for nonprofit organizations. The executive director of Deaf and Hard of Hearing Services was willing to sacrifice her own paycheck to ensure that the other employees were paid. While this is admirable, it was certainly not sustainable in the long run. The agency was on the brink of bankruptcy and needed a business-oriented mindset to survive.

The board needed to shift from a focused social-conscious mindset to a balanced approach that considered both social impact and financial sustainability. We had to make tough decisions—such as selling the building—which allowed us to get rid of a major expense. We also had to focus on growing top-line revenue by building collaborative partnerships with organizations that would hire our services, while we attracted the best interpreters to work for us.

Overall, this story shows that even nonprofit organizations must have a strong business mindset to survive and thrive. They must balance their social mission with solid financial practices to be sustainable for the long term and continue making an impact in their communities.

The story of the agency's hard times cut much deeper for several people who were close to it at the time. As an agency, it finally became clearly understood that you cannot serve the community and fulfill your calling if you can't keep the doors open. Once that clicked, everything else became much clearer.

I believe that whatever you want to see have a long-term impact needs to be sustainable, and that means its financial needs must be tended to with a business mindset. This is true with multinational corporations, just as it is with nonprofits, family businesses, hobbies, vacations, families, and even the person living off-grid on a simple homestead. If you don't get the finances under control, they will control you.

Today, look at the things you depend on and the activities you love. If they are not financially sustainable, look at them with a business mindset, figure out what the problem is, and then fix it. If your mind doesn't work that way, there are many organizations and services that are ready to help you fix the money thing and find peace instead of financial worry.

Mom Dad Not Hear

OH, I KNOW SIGN LANGUAGE

"Although I'm not fluent in sign language by a long way,
I could have a fairly decent conversation."
Paul Theroux, author

Everybody knows a little bit

As an author of children's books, I find myself invited to make school and library visits on a regular basis. I tend to follow the same flow each time: introduction, story reading, discussion questions, teach the students the ABCs in ASL, and then choose some coloring page winners to receive a free autographed copy of my book.

I typically ask many of the same questions at each visit. Early in the discussion, I ask the students, "Which of you knows a Deaf person?" Approximately twenty percent of the students will raise their hands. The follow-up question then is, "Who knows sign language?" Half of the students with their hands up look around and lower their hands. I make a mental note of those who still have their hands raised, and I bank that for the end of my visit.

The best response comes when I tell the students that it's time to learn some sign language. I then ask for a volunteer to stand by me and help me teach the class. I always ask them to lead. If they know the letter sign, they get to share it first. Most students who volunteer are overconfident in what they know, and by the time we hit the letter "E" they start to fumble, so I help them out, taking the lead.

That's how it almost always plays out, until recently. I'm at an elementary school, visiting four groups of third-grade students. In the next to last group, a young lady joins me at the front of the class. She walks up with the same swagger and level of confidence I've seen demonstrated by many other students during this part of the visit. I ask her to start with the letter "A," and she signs it perfectly. Then "B," and again, she nails it. Then "C," "D," and "E." At this point, most kids usually falter, but not her. She continues, demonstrating the correct signs for all 26 letters, without hesitating or missing a beat. It was a show of ASL alphabet perfection! In fact, I'm still surprised, and impressed, as I think back on it months later.

Afterward, I fist-bump her and tell her she's awesome. Then I asked her if she has a Deaf relative. She says, "No, but we have a friend who is Deaf, and a few of us have been learning ASL from books in the library." From the back of the room, her teacher nods, confirming the story.

It becomes very clear why she volunteered. She's confident and willing to bet on herself. Her level of sign language ability isn't the norm for a young kid, especially one who doesn't have a Deaf person in their family. Most people—including adults—who tell you they know some sign language usually know very few signs. But having a Deaf friend had given this young girl the desire to learn and to communicate with her playmate.

When you're confident, bet on yourself

Plenty of people have bet on themselves throughout history...some with good results and others not so good. The young lady who showed her talent in using ASL during my school visit was able to demonstrate the confidence she had in her abilities. She knew exactly how much preparation she had put into learning the language with those library books, and she bet on herself by volunteering to stand in front of her classmates and be tested under pressure. Standing and delivering is a challenge for most adults, let alone a nine-year-old kid.

This girl knew the amount of work she had invested and how much she had prepared, but that doesn't fully explain why she didn't hesitate to put it on the line and bet on herself. She had solid confidence in her abilities, and she was willing to go all in—in front of her classmates—and bet that she could deliver results without folding.

She demonstrated that she was in control of at least that bit of her destiny when she bet on herself.

"But Mickey," you ask, "what about the other three classes in which the students in the same grade and the same school didn't do so well?" Those kids did indeed show great courage by volunteering to stand and deliver. However, the students also came face-to-face with the grim reality of the opposite of succeeding. They stepped up, tried their best, and did OK up to a point, but when the pressure was on, they folded and pushed back from the table. They didn't impress me and their classmates the way they could have, but neither did they completely fail. Their setbacks set them up to become more resilient and to learn from the experience. They came to the solemn realization that they needed to dedicate more effort and time if they wanted to master the ABCs of ASL. I don't doubt that the next time they meet up with a Deaf friend, or stand in front of their class, they'll be better and stronger for having taken the gamble and come up short. Failure isn't forever unless you let it steal your confidence and your will to win. A temporary failure can be the very thing that pushes you to greatness.

Michael Jordan was arguably the greatest basketball player of all time. In a Nike commercial, he once said, "I've missed more than 9,000 shots in my career. I've lost almost 300 games. Twenty-six times, I've been trusted to take the game-winning shot and missed. I've failed over and over and over again in my life. And that is why I succeed."[2]

We typically only see the success stories that result from a person betting on themselves and winning, but often their initial bet could be a failure. Failure is painful, but if we never take the risk to go all in and bet on ourselves, how will we ever know the joy of success?

Really good players sit down at a poker or black-jack table and know the odds of each hand that they have been dealt. But even the best players sometimes ignore the odds and make a bet based on emotion... and that tends to end badly for them. Like a professional gambler, you and I can mitigate the chances of failing when we bet on ourselves. We need to keep a level head. We need to be sure that our confidence in our abilities is well-founded and that we have an accurate assessment of the odds that are stacked against us. If we just rush in and hope for the best, making decisions with our heart and not our head—much like the first few times you played blackjack or poker—you're going to make some very bad bets.

Today, I want you to take some encouragement and admonition from a nine-year-old who demonstrated her success in learning American Sign Language. She walked up to the table, looked at the hand she had been dealt, went all in, and won. You can do the same. A wise person (the quote has been attributed to Thomas Jefferson and others) once said, "The harder I work, the luckier I get."

Today, prepare yourself to be lucky! Do your homework and lead your team fearlessly, giving them the skills, they need to be successful. Build your confidence, practice until winning becomes normal, and then go all in and make that bet on yourself!

PEN AND PAPER

"I was born deaf. I was raised in a hearing world and a deaf world at the same time. I can't say that I like one better than I like the other. I like them both. I speak pretty well; I gesture. If I don't understand something, you know, pen and paper, texting. I use it all."
Sean Berdy, deaf actor, and entrepreneur

Clean-up on Aisle Two

I shake my head in disbelief. Why do I always think it's a good idea to bring the kids along on my mother's weekly trip to the supermarket to stock up on her groceries? It seems like each week something happens to make the trip memorable!

This week, I'm in a hurry. We need to focus and blitz through every section and get out of here in record time. So, I get all managerial and rally the troops. I wave to get my mother's attention, and as she looks at me, I start gesturing. To onlookers—and trust me, when the kids and I show up at the supermarket with my mother, we always draw attention—I'm sure I must look like I'm beside myself. She just nods as I make the ASL signs: "Hurry. Split Up. Shop quickly!"

Things start falling apart immediately. My four-year-old son has already picked out a small kids' shopping cart and is nonchalantly wandering about, pushing the cart into displays and other shoppers. He looks like a cross between a wobbly-legged, newborn calf learning to walk in the pasture and a carnival bumper-car ride. I chase after him as he pushes his tiny shopping cart around, finally stopping him just before he slams into a beautiful display of fresh peaches.

That emergency averted, his focus is now on his grandmother. He can't see her, so he abandons his shopping cart to find out where she has gone. His easy-going adventure has now mushroomed into a life-or-death mission, and he is laser-focused on finding Grandma.

He finally sees her, halfway across the store, standing at the deli counter. He points with excited desperation like an ancient mariner finally spotting land after weeks at sea.

I realize she could probably use some help, so holding my son with one hand and pushing the cart with the other, we weave through the other shoppers and finally step up to my mother's side just as the deli service manager looks at her and asks, "Can I help you, Ma'am?"

I look at her, ready to jump in, and there in my mother's hand is her trusty pen and pad of paper. On the paper is written, "LOW SALT HAM" and the number "2." As she hands the note to the deli man, I know exactly what she wants—low sodium sliced ham, with the meat slicer to be set at number two. She likes the ham to be almost too thin to hold together.

Noticing me, she signs, "Done." And together we head to the cashier. Finally, and miraculously, we all manage to unite back in the car, almost on schedule.

I really didn't know what my mother kept in her purse. I always felt weird touching her purse, let alone looking into it! I was pretty sure that she carried some basic makeup and a small package of tissues in there. I had also seen her sneak some hard candy out of it and slip it to the kids when she thought I wasn't looking. But I knew for certain that she always had a pen and a small pad of paper in that purse, and many times—like at the deli counter—it was the only way she could accurately communicate what she wanted.

Most people that she needed to interact with didn't know her language. Of course, they would try speaking to her in English, and not getting a response, they would speak slower and louder, which didn't help. She'd look at them, shake her head, tap her ear, and finally open her purse and write a note. The utter simplicity of ink on paper never failed to get her message across.

Great people always find a way

I have always admired people who faced adversity, but worked hard and found a way to overcome the odds and succeed. The "Greats" always seem to find a way to win. I remember hearing a story about the legendary football coach Vince Lombardi. His team, the Green Bay Packers, had lost the championship game the preceding year. When they gathered for the first day of training camp the following season, the future Hall of Fame coach held up a football and said, "Gentlemen, this is a football." The coach took his team back to page one of the playbook and focused on fundamentals. They went on to win the championship, that year and five in the next seven years. Great people find a way to win.

In my career, I've been surrounded by people of all performance levels. Some were fine with being part of the herd, not standing out, but not falling behind either. Others just could not be held back. I realized that those who were destined for greatness had an uncanny ability to evaluate whatever difficult situation they found themselves in and somehow make a way to create a winning outcome.

Coach Lombardi took the Green Bay Packers back to the very basic fundamentals of football and created a dynasty. My mother faced the daily hardship of communicating in a hearing world by also going back to the basics of pen and paper. Lombardi and my mother were on far different playing fields, but they're both greats, and both created winning outcomes.

Today, I want to encourage you to approach everything you do with the realization that you have a shot at leadership and greatness. Some of us are business leaders. We have responsibility for a team, a department, a division, or even a corporation. Many of us are parents. We have the responsibility as a father or mother to lead a family. Teachers and professors lead students. I hope you get this: Every element of your life gives you a shot at leadership and greatness. Don't look at your problems and complain about the obstacles life is throwing at you. Take charge and be a leader—even if you're only taking responsibility for yourself. This is your shot at greatness. Today, face your problems, go back to basics, create solutions, and find a way to win.

Mom Dad Not Hear

MONEY MATTERS

"Deaf people in low-income communities face a double disadvantage: they're often the poorest of the poor and the most marginalized of the marginalized."
Carol Padden, author and professor

Arguing about money

The scene was often the same. My sister and I would be watching television in our living room when we would hear a conversation start to get animated at the kitchen table. Our childhood home was small and cramped, roughly 1,200 square feet in size, with three bedrooms and one bath. There was very little privacy, so you heard everything happening everywhere.

Nine times out of ten, those conflicts in the kitchen were because of some money issue. My mother was the more financially conservative of my parents, and she took charge of handling the family finances. Her main challenge was trying to limit my father's spending.

These discussions frequently grew into heated arguments, and I hated hearing them. I didn't under-stand the details of what was behind the problems my parents were dealing with, but I knew from an early age that problems with money were to be avoided like the plague. I witnessed the stress and emotional pain that accompany not having enough money, and I didn't want to be guilty of inflicting that on anybody I loved. It's a lesson I'm glad I learned, and it has shaped my work ethic, my drive for success, and the way I think. I'm a better person because of it.

I am not so naive to think that household financial problems were unique to my Deaf parents. Money issues are a major source of conflict in many families, but research shows that Deaf people are hit especially hard. In my limited spare time, serving on the board of directors for D&HHS, a recurring issue that we discuss is the financial challenge that so many Deaf people experience.

It's not that the ability to hear makes people more fiscally responsible. Instead, the inability to hear greatly impacts performance in school, and there is often a direct correlation between education and economic success.

In 2008, Barbara Gerner de Garcia and Rosalinda B. Barrera authored a report called *Deaf People and Economic Well-Being: A Research Summary.*[3] This report summarized the findings of several studies on the economic well-being of Deaf people in the United Kingdom. The studies found that Deaf people have higher rates of poverty and unemployment than the general population, and that access to education and training is a key factor in their economic success or failure.

When I look back at those arguments at the kitchen table, I realize that my mother and father had two very different financial perspectives, but they did agree on one thing—they despised not having enough money. Unfortunately, they had completely opposite philosophies about how they should fix that problem. My father thought the solution was to make more money. My mother believed the best way to have money was to spend less and save more.

If they had stopped arguing long enough to have a reasonable discussion, they would have realized that both of them were right. They needed to focus on both strategies. To have enough money, they needed to maximize their income and minimize their expenses.

Maximize, minimize, build

My parents made an indelible impact on my feelings about money, and they never knew it. As I matured, I vowed to be in a strong enough financial position so that every little purchase wouldn't prompt an argument with my wife. What I perceived in observing my parents was that only holding to one part of the financial equation wasn't sufficient.

For our household to avoid the kind of arguments I lived through as a young boy, my wife and I agreed on this ideology: "maximize, minimize, build." We are firmly committed to maximizing our income, minimizing our expenses, and building something that can make the first two stronger and more successful.

The idea of, "maximize, minimize, build" is nothing new. It's standard practice in many disciplines—finance, management, engineering, and others. This formula has helped us handle our family finances with far less drama than I experienced growing up. In addition, I've found that it has helped me in the leadership roles I've held in the corporate world.

But how do you actually do it? Here are a few ways:

1. **MAXIMIZE** your income. The most obvious way to increase your personal or family income is to get a better-paying job, but there are other ways as well. You can try to negotiate a raise or look for side gigs to earn extra income. In a corporate setting, this relates to helping your department or team maximize its receivables—selling more services or products, setting a higher profit margin, or finding new sources of income.

2. **MAXIMIZE** your emergency funds. Setting aside a portion of your income for emergencies can help you avoid the panic and stress of spending money you don't have. At the office, ensure you have both contingency and reserves set aside on every project.

3. **MAXIMIZE** by creating a budget. A budget is a great way to keep track of your income and expenses. Create a realistic budget and stick to it as closely as

possible. This is important in your family, as well as in your business.

4. MINIMIZE your debt. If you have debt—in addition to your mortgage—you should be laser-focused on getting rid of it. Paying off debt reduces your expenses in the long run and maximizes money for other purposes. In business, some debt is normal, but it needs to be managed and kept within a manageable level.

5. MINIMIZE your outgo by tracking your spending. Most people believe they spend less than they actually do. Keep track of your spending so your budget can reflect reality. You can do this using a spreadsheet or a budgeting app. Typically businesses do a great job of tracking expenses but be sure that your team monitors all expenses, so you know what gets passed on to the client or customer and what eats into your profit.

6. MINIMIZE your expenses. Review your budget considering what you spend and then identify areas where you can cut back. This may include eating out less, reducing entertainment expenses, or shopping for less expensive brands. Examine your team's expense guidelines ensuring that travel, entertainment, or personal growth expenses do not get out of hand.

7. BUILD a business. Look at your skills and passions. Starting an income-generating operation can result in phenomenal personal and financial growth. This is how you can realize your full financial potential. You can help your company find additional ways to monetize the services or products that you already provide.

8. BUILD your personal brand. The image people have of you and your business is important, so take the time to define it. Building your personal brand can help increase visibility and attract higher-paying clients or customers. This could involve creating a website, growing your social media presence, or showcasing your expertise and offerings in community involvement. This is important for you to work on in your business life as well. Find ways to expand the company's image and brand in the community. Look for ways to insert your team into nonprofit or social service opportunities so you are seen as giving generously.

9. BUILD your network. Take this to the bank— your net worth is your network. Building a strong professional network can lead to new job opportunities, mentorship, partnerships, and referrals that can open doors to new clients or customers. This works in both your personal and professional life.

Today, take your role as a leader seriously and examine the ways you can "maximize, minimize, and build" for your future. Be sure you're actively working on all three parts of that strategy.

THIRTY YEARS AND KICKED OUT

"What gunpowder did for war the printing press has done for the mind."
Wendell Phillips, abolitionist, advocate, orator, and attorney

The print shop

It's the middle of a workday, I'm in my office and my phone chirps. I glance over and notice a text message has just arrived from my father. I finish what I am doing and pick up the phone. Opening the text message, I notice it's a photo of a letter on his company stationery. I see the name and phone number of my father's union steward, along with the official notice that my father's job had just ended.

I still have a busy day ahead of me, so I quickly reply to my father's text message. I try to give him some assurance, "Stay calm, Dad. Don't worry. You'll be OK. I love you, and I'll Skype with you from home tonight."

I rush home as soon as I can, sit at my computer, and log onto Skype to talk with him face-to-face. Staring at me through the computer screen I see a man I had never seen before. This big powerful man looked beaten down, unnerved, hurt, and lost. The day had started like any other workday for him, but in a moment's time, everything changed. It was so sudden. I could only imagine how he felt. Talking with my dad—both of us signing rapidly—my head was spinning. I never saw this coming and obviously, neither did my father. The world which he had known for thirty years came to a screeching halt without any warning.

This change wasn't sitting well with him at all. This isn't how he imagined his career as a printing press technician ending. There would be no retirement party with his work friends. There was nothing to celebrate.

My father had been a good employee, and he knew it. Unfortunately, his employer was downsizing and had decided to get rid of the on-site printing operation and outsource their future printing needs. That offset printing press had been my father's office for thirty years.

I can still remember visiting that print shop as a boy like it was yesterday. As soon as anyone would walk in, an obnoxious orange strobe light would start flashing, notifying my father that someone was there. The press was housed in a green outbuilding, about 200 yards from the administration offices. It's no wonder the administration didn't want it any closer—the smell was awful.

The ink and especially the solvents used to clean the ink off the press, combined to form a pungent and somewhat acrid odor. Additionally, the paper stock often contributed to the scent. If it was fresh from the mill, it had a strong woody or pulpy aroma. Overall, the smell of a printing press would often irritate people when they got their first whiff, but for those who have spent years in a print shop, it can be a familiar and nostalgic scent, bringing back fond memories.

It's not just the smell that makes a print shop a challenging work environment; it's also the noise. When the press is running, it can be loud, very loud. That's why many Deaf people were hired to work in printing press operations. It makes perfect sense because Deaf employees are not fazed by the noise. As I think back, I'd estimate that probably half of my parents' Deaf friends worked in print shops.

But on that day, thirty years of smelly and noisy employment and hard work came to an end for my father. Thirty years and kicked out. It was a grim reminder to my father—and to me—that loyalty doesn't stay with a company. Loyalty follows people, for better or for worse.

Loyalty comes from people... not a company

I was in my thirties and had already established myself in a good job with a best-in-class corporation when my father was laid off. I didn't know what to do or what to say. I had never experienced anyone close to me losing a job. That may seem unbelievable, but I come from a lineage of loyal employees. Without exception, every member of my immediate family has been with the same employer for a significant amount of time. My mother was leading the charge after 42 years with the same employer, my father had 30 years, my sister has been with one company for nearly 20 years, and I have been with the same organization now for 23 years and counting. Loyalty is in our blood.

Since seeing my father go through his layoff, I've seen many colleagues and friends being transferred or laid off. It is never easy—period. It is always a hard, painful blow to a person's identity, confidence, ego, and self-worth.

Studies have shown that employees who *feel* loyal to their organization are more likely to say their job gives them satisfaction and to stay with the company for a longer period of time. These people will work harder and be more committed to the success of the organization.

When I look at why people are loyal and remain with one employer for a significant amount of time, I believe that the main reason is not because of the company, but rather it's because of the people they work with at that company. They can become like a family.

Loyalty is a two-way street. Employers must demonstrate loyalty to their employees by providing a positive work environment, competitive compensation, and opportunities for growth and development. When employers fail to show loyalty to their employees, it can lead to decreased morale, increased turnover, and ultimately it can hurt the organization's bottom line.

Leaders who prioritize loyalty and strive to create a mutually beneficial relationship with their team members are more likely to see positive outcomes in their employees' job satisfaction, productivity, and retention. They create loyalty on their team.

Great leaders demonstrate daily that loyalty is a quality they value and practice. When that takes place, the magic happens, and you end up with a team of people who are so loyal, that they will run through a wall for you. Today, show your team that you prioritize loyalty!

LESSONS FROM PART ONE
LEADERSHIP

1   **The best leaders communicate clearly.** Be sensitive to the people you lead. Think about your hearer's needs and state of mind, and vary your style of communication to fit the mood and personality of your listener.

2   **Good intentions only go so far.** Lead by example, build trust, and model for your team the values and behaviors you are hoping to see developed in them. Actions are more important than words. So, stop *intending* to do good, and just do it.

3   **Pay attention to the signals around you—have situational awareness.** Use this input to make educated decisions and adjust quickly. Great leaders move rapidly from observation to action, allowing them to create a solution before others realize there is a problem.

4   **Don't let yourself get distracted.** Noise is all around you and often inside your head as well. Take control of your thoughts and learn to focus on what's most important. Don't let yourself get sidetracked from accomplishing your goals.

5

Learn to be a chameleon. Adjust to your surroundings—be flexible! Start by embracing and strengthening your multiple skills and abilities. As you become a versatile leader, be nimble to adapt to various situations and challenges. You don't need to stand out in a crowd to be a good leader. Let yourself be invisible, if that's what it takes to get the job done well.

6

To have an enduring positive impact, the things you value must be sustainable—their financial needs must be tended to with a business mindset. If you don't get the finances under control, they will control you.

7

Bet on yourself! It takes courage and determination to develop the skills needed to lead your team fearlessly. Build your confidence, practice until winning becomes normal, and have the courage and grit to trust yourself and believe you can win. And don't fear failure. It can give you the motivation you need to keep improving and succeed next time.

8

Find solutions—that's what great leaders do. Approach everything you do with the realization that you have a shot at leadership and greatness. Whether it's in a corporation, your own business, or in a family, there's always a way to succeed. Just don't give up!

9 To help you master your money matters follow this formula: "maximize, minimize, build." Become firmly committed to maximizing your income, minimizing your expenses, and building something that can make the first two stronger and more successful.

10 Rise above disappointment. People you expect to be loyal are going to let you down. But you can demonstrate loyalty to those above you and below you. Leaders who value loyalty work to create a mutually beneficial relationship with their team members, and in so doing, they create loyalty on their team.

PART TWO

LIFE

Mom Dad Not Hear

CONVERSATIONS WITH TELEMARKETERS

"No one is as deaf as the man who will not listen."
Jewish Proverb

They will still be deaf tomorrow

It was a constant source of irritation. Throughout the evening, no matter what I found myself doing, the phone would keep ringing. As you've already learned, I was the one who usually answered the phone in our house. Often, it was a telemarketer calling to talk my parents into buying something.

By the time I reached my teenage years, I had learned a thing or two about phone etiquette. My infamous "Mom, Dad not Hear" police incident showed me I needed to add some finesse and skill to my telephone responses. I also learned early on that I was not a fan of telemarketers. Here's how I would try to handle those phone conversations:

Mickey: "Hello, this is Mickey."

Telemarketer: "Good evening, is Mr. or Mrs. Carolan there?

Mickey: "Yes, they are here, but they are Deaf and cannot speak with you. I can relay a message if you would like."

Telemarketer: "May I ask who I am speaking with?"

Mickey: "This is their son, Mickey."

Telemarketer: "Are you over 18?"

Mickey: "No, I am not, but I have their permission to relay the message."

Telemarketer: "Thank you, Mickey, but we will call back tomorrow."

Mickey: "Sir, they will still be Deaf tomorrow, so unfortunately, we'll have this same conversation if you call again. It may be best if you put us on your 'Do not call' list."

Telemarketer: "Oh, OK, sure, I can do that."

That was one version of a call. The other version was when they misunderstood the word "Deaf" and thought I said, "dead." It was never intentional, as I was sure it must be terrible juju to say your parents were dead. That mix-up would often lead to the telemarketer saying, "Oh, I'm so sorry for your loss. I'll take them off my list." So, while I feared there might be some bad karma to deal with, at least it got the desired result!

Know how to pronounce names correctly

When telemarketers would call and butcher our last name, that immediately flagged them as someone I didn't want to talk with for very long. The same goes for people we encounter in our daily lives. You've probably experienced the same feeling when someone mispronounces your name or calls you the wrong name altogether. That feeling should instruct you to be sure you don't treat other people the same way. If your interaction with someone starts with you messing up their name, their thoughts turn negative, their attention span subconsciously shrinks, and whatever message you were trying to relay becomes far less effective. Maya Angelou, the influential poet, said it well, "I've learned that people will forget what you said, people will forget what you did, but people will never forget how you made them feel." When you butcher a person's name, it is an insult and results in a negative feeling that sticks with them.

One of the most respectful things you can do in life is to learn people's names and find out how to pronounce them correctly. On the opposite end of the spectrum, if you just wing it and call someone the wrong name or mispronounce it, you'll never make up for that poor first impression. While many people with a name that's tough to pronounce are used to it, and will often laugh it off, they still associate it with a lack of respect.

It has never been easier to figure out how to pronounce someone's name with technology at our fingertips. So, I implore you, starting today, when you meet someone new, listen carefully to hear how they pronounce their name, and then remember it for the next time you see them.

By the way, in the event you might be wondering, my last name is enunciated as CARE-Olin. Now, you don't need to mispronounce it when you recommend this book to a friend!

WELCOME TO COLLEGE, FRESHMAN

*"The only thing standing between you and
your goal is the story you keep telling yourself
as to why you can't achieve it."*
Jordan Belfort, entrepreneur, speaker, and author

Boer-Bennink Dorm

It's a hot summer day, the last weekend in August. I'm feeling good, ready to start the next chapter in my life. I've just celebrated my eighteenth birthday, so now, legally, I'm an adult. I'm packing the last of my things into my 1993 Chevy Cavalier (my parents had sold it to me for $1,000 for reliable transportation on trips home from college). I realize how fast things are moving and changing. In just a few hours, I'll be sharing a dorm room with a guy named David, my assigned roommate.

My parents and I drive the three-hour trip from Fairgrove to Grand Rapids. They are in their car and I'm driving mine.

We pull into the entrance of Calvin College and drive to the visitor parking lot behind my residence hall, the Boer-Bennink dorm. Despite being just before Labor Day, summer has shown up in full force. As we make many trips back and forth from the parking lot to my dorm room, we all sweat profusely. We keep busy unloading my car and carrying the many boxes and bags into my dorm room.

I'm already doing my best to fit in with the campus culture. My parents are trying to keep their emotions under control. The magnitude of what is happening hasn't really hit me just yet. I find myself thinking, selfishly, that finally, I'll have the chance to lead a normal life on my own. I know my sister will step up and interpret for my parents while I'm away.

I think about my mother and father. They have huge dreams for my sister and me. This step—me going off to college—is a big deal for them, too. I know it's validation that they are good parents, and despite being Deaf, that they're raising successful children just as well as any hearing parents, if not better. Helping me move into college is part of that proof.

But the fall semester of my freshman year turned out to be quite different than any of us expected. Looking back, the mere fact that I survived such a rollercoaster of events and emotions was evidence that I had the grit to stick it out. It sure didn't feel like it at the time. The first major hurdle was Chaos Day. This Calvin tradition pits dorm against dorm in various physical, athletic, and mental challenges. It demands all-in participation from every resident, and the winning dorm gets huge bragging rights for the entire year. My first Chaos Day started by hearing the resident assistants running through the dorm hallways, banging pots and pans to wake everyone up.

But I was already awake—I'd been up for hours with a splitting headache, throbbing tooth pain, and a fever. Clearly, I wasn't going to be participating in Chaos Day. I was having my own chaos! Instead of fun competitive events, I found myself in the office of an unfamiliar dentist, having an emergency root canal. It was a Saturday, and I can't recall how I found a dentist who would agree to see me. It was a minor miracle, and despite the discomfort, I remember being so glad that I didn't have to endure that pain all weekend.

After the Chaos Day emergency root canal, college wasn't turning out to be the constant fun and games that I had hoped it would be. I had sailed through high school, but I quickly realized that Calvin was nothing like my small-town high school. I was no longer a big fish in a small pond. It was shocking to face the reality of my poor study habits. I needed to find more hours each day for schoolwork. Late-night sessions in the computer lab became the norm (these computer labs were located in dorms and classroom buildings back when very few of us had our own computers).

Just when I started to get a rhythm going with my studies, another disaster hit me. I had a girlfriend back in my senior year of high school, and she had been planning for years to attend Calvin College. Yes, I followed her to the university so we could be on the same campus together. Now, in our first semester of college, she decided to break up with me. My heart was shattered, and my head was spinning, but I didn't have time to feel badly for myself—tryouts for the baseball team were coming up. I just HAD to be selected to play on the varsity baseball team! That girl was the first reason I was here, and baseball was a very close second!

I had a solid tryout; I worked hard and did my best. But to make a bad first year even worse, I didn't make the team. The head coach told me my arm wasn't strong enough. I dragged myself back to my dorm room and just lost it. Tears started flowing and my mind was spinning, trying to figure out what was next. I knew I had to call home and tell my parents what happened. I had to admit that it seemed like every reason I had for attending college had fallen apart.

It was 8:00 P.M., my sister had just gotten home from basketball practice, and she picked up the phone when I called. Only a few weeks previous, I made a similar call to tell my parents that my girlfriend had broken up with me. Now, here I was again, calling with bad news—I hadn't been chosen for the baseball team.

I told my sister, so she would translate it into American Sign Language for my parents to know what I was saying. I could hear my parents in the background and knew they were having a spirited discussion. I asked my sister, "What are they saying?" She tried to downplay it, "Oh, nothing. They're just talking." I knew better, "What are they saying?" I asked again.

Finally, my sister came clean, "Well, Dad says you should drop out of Calvin and come home and go to Saginaw Valley State University." I could see how that might make sense to him, but I replied, "No, I am finishing the year, and we can discuss it more this summer when I'm home." In the space of just a few tense minutes, I had made the important decision to stick it out. I decided that I wasn't going to quit. Looking back, I was hurting when I made the call to tell them the disappointing news, hoping for sympathy and support from them. Instead, it was a wake-up call that helped me discover a trifecta of life lessons.

That phone call marked a crucial point for me. I realized that I was at a crossroads. I had a decision to make—I could quit and start going in a new direction, or I could continue straight ahead on the same road I was already traveling. Looking back, I realize that was a decisive, defining moment, marking the point where I started making my own decisions and living my own life. It also brought my father some needed clarity. He had been struggling with my being three hours away at college and not being able to interpret for him. He now had to rely on my sister, who wasn't as strong an interpreter. At that moment, my father determined he would find the necessary grit to figure out how to carry on with my sister as his interpreter.

A trifecta of life lessons

That freshman year helped me build character. It was a difficult time, but I emerged wiser and more resolute. I realized there were some very good reasons why I chose to attend Calvin. It wasn't just following a girl to a school where I could play college baseball. In my mind, playing baseball in college would impress my father and further polish my legacy back home in Fairgrove.

Instead, I came to realize that I had enrolled at Calvin because I was looking for a different perspective on life, away from my hometown. I knew there was a very big world out there that I needed to experience, and for a small-town boy, moving nearly three hours away was a good way to start. I finally understood that I needed to grow as a person—physically, mentally, and spiritually—and Calvin was a great school for enhancing those three dimensions of my life. I also realized I needed to be much more self-sufficient. That was a rude awakening for a kid whose mother had been cooking his meals and washing his clothes just months before.

When I think about my freshman year, it is a wonder that I made it. Now, the adult Mickey looks back at that moment and realizes it was an important part of growing up. Life brings certain unplanned—and often unwanted—events for a reason.

I believe they happened to me because I needed to learn grit and how to work through hardships and emotions by myself, not relying on an environment of safety back home. The adversity helped shape me into who I am today. Through it, I learned and grew a lot.

Here they are, my trifecta of life lessons learned that freshman year: Number One—don't make life decisions based on what your high school sweetheart decides to do. Odds are it won't end well. Number Two—College athletics have a way of humbling you. That's not a bad thing. It can make you work all the harder and not be so impressed with yourself. And Number Three—don't quit when you hit a few roadblocks. Put your chin down and keep going.

Today, I hope everything goes well for you, but I'm realistic enough to know that it probably won't. There is a good chance that something in your life will not go as planned. Don't look at the speed bumps on the road of life as permanent roadblocks. Get your bearings, recalculate what your next steps should be, and whatever you do, don't quit!

INTERPRETING: CODAS VS. PROFESSIONALS

"Many people do not understand the role of the interpreter, don't really value the importance. We're talking about somebody's life. If the interpretation is not done correctly, big mistakes can be made."
Guillermo Arenas, Interpreter

A CODA's Perspective

Join me for a conversation at the Carolan family dinner table. I'm talking with my daughter Elloree, who's telling me about her latest adventures as a first grader...

Elloree: "Dad, I know how to sign colors in sign language."

Mickey: "Oh really? Show me, please."

Elloree: "This is red." She makes a fist and opens her index finger by pointing upwards. She brings the finger in front of her chin and slides it down.

Mickey: "Awesome! That's correct. What other colors do you know?"

Elloree: "This is blue." She makes a "B" letter sign in sign language
and shakes her hand back and forth.

Mickey: "Right as rain! What else?"

Elloree: "This is white." She proceeds to face her palm towards her chest with her thumb extended and pulls her hand away while closing her fingers.

Mickey: "Great job! Keep going."

Elloree: "This is purple." She makes a "P" letter sign in sign language

and twists it back and forth.

Mickey: "That's not purple; this is purple." I flick my middle finger multiple times under my chin.

Elloree: "NO, that's not the sign that Meekah showed on YouTube!"

Mickey: "Well, Meekah is wrong! I've been signing for over 40 years."

Elloree: "Then, you've been doing it wrong forever."

Mickey: "OK, I'm going to look it up on my phone." And I proceed to search for it on my phone. Dang. Elloree is right. I have just lost an argument with a six-year-old. I look up from my phone and say, "Just a minute, I'm going to call your Grandma."

I proceed to call my mother on her cell phone. Soon she appears on my screen for a video chat so we can communicate with ASL. I get right to the point and tell her she taught me the wrong sign for purple, and it's her fault that I just lost an argument with my daughter. I lose enough arguments on my own—I surely don't need her help!

American Sign Language was my first language. It's what I learned from my mother and father at home, the way most American kids learn English. But unlike those other kids who also studied English in school, I never had any classes in ASL. I watched, copied the signs that I saw being used, and figured out what they all meant. It's no wonder that I'd get a word wrong every now and then!

It was a necessity for me to quickly become proficient in American Sign Language, because my parents needed an interpreter they could rely on every day. I began interpreting for them from a very young age. While I never received any formal training in interpretation and never earned any certifications, I was able to help my parents communicate with the hearing world—a responsibility and a privilege that I am proud to have fulfilled throughout my life.

A professional ASL interpreter, on the other hand, is someone who has completed formal training in American Sign Language and English and has expert fluency in both. They have also learned the ethical and legal requirements of interpretation and have achieved certification through a recognized interpreting organization, such as the Registry of Interpreters for the Deaf (RID). Professional ASL interpreters are trained to interpret back-and-forth between ASL and spoken English, and they often work in a variety of settings, such as schools, government agencies, hospitals, courts, and businesses. They adhere to a code of ethics and are held to high professional standards of conduct and confidentiality.

Over the years, I have come to realize a very critical difference between how I interpret for my parents and how professionals handle that role. Certified professionals are required to interpret *everything* that is being said. They are legally and morally obligated to interpret each word. I was not bound by that obligation. So, I usually did not interpret everything that was being said. I only interpreted the message or the meaning of the message that I judged to be necessary and important at that moment.

As I've matured, my proficiency at interpretation has grown as my skill in communication has developed. I have gotten much better at conveying the nuances of a conversation delivered using sign language. I remember many times as a teenager I would say, "Don't worry about it, Dad" or "I'll tell you everything they said later." That might work for a kid casually telling his parents what people are saying, but ethically, that is a cardinal sin in the interpreting world.

"Don't worry about it," or "I'll tell you what they said later," was the unprofessional side of my rudimentary CODA interpretation. But the positive side was my ability to interpret for my parents in a way that added context and understanding to what they were saying during the interpreted conversation.

Providing that filtering and reasoning often helped to mitigate what could have become emotionally charged responses by my parents.

I am glad that I am strong enough in both English and ASL that I can communicate clearly to any Deaf person, and I can be an effective and skillful interpreter for my mother when she needs me but, I'm not a pro.

When in doubt, always hire a professional

I'm a guy. I like to think that I'm proficient at many things. For much of my life, I was a real proponent of the "do it yourself" self-sufficient mentality. I have a pretty good track record at it, too! But as I've matured, I've realized the value of hiring professionals—and appreciating their expertise. Think about some of the services you expect to be done correctly and well:

• Haircuts and hair color. after one too many "OK" box dye jobs, you understand the wisdom of booking a professional to do it right, unless you're bald like me.

• House painting. after repainting a room repeatedly and failing to get the line straight where the wall meets the ceiling, you hire a professional to do it right the first time.

• Oil change. after you forgot to tighten the drain plug, resulting in your oil leaking out and almost ruining your engine, having a pro do the job doesn't seem such a bad deal.

I'm sure you've experienced something similar. You start to do something yourself but realize it would be better if you hired someone really good at it—a professional. There are so many benefits to hiring someone who knows what they're doing. You get a job done faster, better, and with far fewer headaches than if you had stubbornly determined that you would do it yourself. And perhaps the biggest benefit is that you get to keep your most precious commodity—time.

Regaining my time is what finally convinced me to begin hiring professionals to do my DIY tasks. Look at it this way—if it takes you an hour every week to mow your lawn, hiring a professional to do it for you would give you back 52 hours each year to do something you would rather do. Of course, if you don't live in a place where your lawn grows year-round then you'll probably save even more time by hiring a professional to plow the snow in your driveway!

There are also quality, efficiency, and legal reasons for hiring a professional. When my mother has an important meeting with her medical doctor, professional interpreters who know the correct medical terms will quickly differentiate themselves and demonstrate why you want a pro interpreter in this complex environment. Their medical endorsement and ability to flawlessly interpret anything the doctor says prove that they are professionals.

Today, if you see something that you are tempted to DIY, stop and ask yourself if there might be a professional who could do it faster and better so that you can put that time to another use? If there is, then let me advise you to seriously consider using the professional! Use the time you save to make a difference in your life, or in another person's life, that only you can do.

Mom Dad Not Hear

A FULFILLING CUSTOMER VISIT

*"I try to talk to everybody. If you can't speak
English, I'm going to do sign language."*
Helen Wilson Nies, former chief judge
US Court of Appeals

This almost seems like a setup

It's an October morning, in Northern Michigan. I'm finishing up my hotel breakfast while I wait for another member of the sales team to arrive, so we can prepare for our customer meeting later that morning. Dave arrives on time, as usual, and he gives me a rundown on the account. Mid-way through the conversation, his briefing takes a unique turn:

Dave: "When we are at the client site, you may see some employees walk in and out of the place where we'll be meeting. In fact, they may kind of look at you and nod their head without saying anything."

Mickey: "Really? Why is that?"

Dave: "Well, it's because they probably won't understand who you are or what we are talking about. I've discovered some Deaf employees work there, including the owner's brother and the vice president."

Mickey (with a smirk on my face): "Dave, that's amazing! Did you know both of my parents are Deaf, and I'm fluent in sign language?"

Dave (with a perplexed look): "No way. You're kidding me, right?"

Mickey: "No. It's the truth."

Dave (laughing): "This is almost going to seem like a setup that I'm bringing you along on this customer visit with me!"

After the briefing, we drive to the customer's location. After the initial small talk, Dave happens to bring up that I know sign language, and although it's surprising, the news is received very well by the owner of the company. I jump in and tell some stories about growing up with Deaf parents. Then the owner's brother walks up and introduces himself—using ASL. We launch into a conversation that only a couple of people in the room understand.

As we take a tour of the company, we encounter other Deaf employees who are friendly and greet me verbally. I return their smiles and catch them completely off guard by responding in their language and having short conversations in ASL.

For a few months, that story took on a life of its own internally within our company. Everyone was fascinated, not only that I was fluent in sign language, but that I ended up in a situation where I could use it during a customer visit.

Learn another language

I had prepared well for that customer visit—as I always do. I arrived at the hotel the night before and had gotten a good night's rest. I had a healthy breakfast and a good briefing with my associate. But never in my wildest dreams did I imagine that this sales call would have taken this incredible route. This isn't the only time I've been able to use ASL while conducting business, but it was certainly one of the most memorable.

Whether you're like me and English is your second language, or if you grew up speaking English and you've worked diligently to learn an additional language, there is usually a very good reason why you did the work to be able to communicate in another language. Maybe you moved to a new country or married into a family that speaks another language. Whatever it was, beyond that initial reason, you never really know when you're going to use it.

For example, I know that when I talk to my mother, we'll be using ASL. That is 95 percent of the time that I use it, and the remaining 5 percent would be when I'm at a Deaf social event or board meeting. Otherwise, I rarely find any use for my knowledge of ASL. But what I do know is that at any given time I need to be ready to communicate, and without any thought or preparation, I may need to do it using sign language. All the time, I need to be ready to have a conversation with someone who isn't a native English speaker. We all need to know how we can communicate with someone who does not share our language.

It's never too late to start learning another language. Becoming bilingual has been shown to improve your "executive functions," which are the most complex brain processes. The term "executive functions" describes the skills that allow you to control, direct, and manage your attention, as well as your ability to plan. A bilingual person has mastery of two languages, and that requires constantly managing the interference of the languages so that she or he doesn't say the wrong word in the wrong language at the wrong time. Executive functions also help you ignore irrelevant information and distractions to focus on what's important.[4]

In fact, the volume of gray matter has been shown to be greater in study participants who spoke both English and another language, compared to participants who spoke only English. Bilingualism also affects the white matter of our brains, allowing messages to travel faster and more efficiently across networks of nerves to reach the brain. And being bilingual promotes the integrity of your brain as you age. It gives you more neurons, and it strengthens or maintains the connections between them so that communication can happen optimally.[5] So if you want to stay young and alert as you get older, I recommend that you begin to learn another language today, and find somebody who speaks it!

HUNTING

When he was young, I told Dale Jr. that hunting and racing are a lot alike. Holding that steering wheel and holding that rifle both mean you better be responsible.
Dale Earnhardt, NASCAR Hall of Fame driver

If you want to shoot a deer, don't hunt with a Deaf person

November 15th is an unofficial holiday in Michigan, particularly in rural Michigan. It's the opening day of firearm deer season. Hunting off the land has been in my mother's family's blood since the beginning of time. My father, having joined the family by marriage, took up hunting later as an adult.

In the evening of each opening day, I would interpret the same message from my dad to my uncles: "Neighbor is too close; scare deer away." However, here is the truth about what happened that day in the blind to scare the deer away:

5:00 A.M.: Wake up and load up my father's blue Dodge Ram pickup truck.

5:30 A.M.: Arrive at the farm my uncles owned.

6:00 A.M.: Drive part-way down the fence row and walk the remainder of the way to the hunting blind.

6:30 A.M.: The propane heater would be running, and we'd be settled in.

6:45 A.M.: Dad would cough, not knowing how loud he was.

7:22 A.M.: Sunrise, we were fully alert, looking for moving deer.

7:30 A.M.: Dad would cough again, still not realizing how loud he sounded.

8:00 A.M.: Shots fired. Not us—the neighbor—who successfully harvested a deer.

8:30 A.M.: Dad would start getting worked up, seeing the neighboring hunter moving around outside of his blind, working on the deer he harvested.

9:00 A.M.: Time for a snack, Dad makes more noise unwrapping his sandwich loudly.

9:30 A.M.: Time for a leak. Dad steps out of the blind, breaking twigs, and takes a leak.

10:00 A.M.: A trio of does runs from neighboring woods; they cross within shooting distance. Dad gets worked up again because, on our uncle's property, there is a rule that we do not shoot a doe.

10:30 A.M.: Dad coughs loudly yet again.

11:00 A.M.: "No more deer, go home," Dad would dramatically sign, and I'd interpret.

11:30 A.M.: We're eating lunch in Grandma Jackson's house, while everyone else stays in their blinds.

Noon: Nap time

3:00 P.M.: Load back up and settle back in the blind for the afternoon hunt.

4:00 P.M.: Nature calls, time for a leak.

5:00 P.M.: Dad opens a large pop bottle that fizzes, making too much noise.

5:15 P.M.: The sun sets, ending the day of hunting—with no deer shot.

It was no coincidence that the only bucks I harvested during my youth came as the result of sitting in the blind without my father. I was a terrible shot and missed more than I hit. However, since I knew the problems that accompany making noise—and was cognizant of when I was making sounds—I was able to wait for the deer to come into range, and have a shot at them more successfully.

Now, before anyone gets argumentative that Deaf people can't hunt, I'll readily acknowledge that there are exceptions to the rule—but my dad wasn't one of them. I've learned that even the best Deaf hunters are at a disadvantage when hunting wild game. Most successful Deaf hunters rely on hearing guides or have worked diligently to mitigate as many of the disadvantages that come from not being able to hear in the wild.

Do not disturb the woods

If you want to hunt deer, you're going to need to go where the deer are—which is in or near the woods. A primary lesson I learned while hunting was not to disturb the woods. I saw firsthand from multiple blind sits with my father that the wrong noise or scent could reveal our presence and ruin the entire day. When moving amongst the trees and undergrowth found in the woods, the deer will usually see, hear, or smell you long before you spot them.

I've had my best success in the woods when I stayed off the land I would later be hunting on as much as I could in the off-season and left it as a natural habitat for the deer and other woodland creatures. I'm no hunting expert, but I know this much—my best chance at being successful in the woods is if I am careful to not leave my imprint on it. When that happens, even if the deer detect that I am nearby, they will be much quicker to calm down and resume their natural movement patterns if they don't continue picking up my scent and seeing additional evidence of my presence in their home environment.

Get prepared, and be patient

So many lessons I've learned while hunting apply to other areas of life. I've learned that preparation is primary and patience is paramount. If you want to be a successful deer hunter, patience is a mandatory virtue. Deer seldom appear on your preferred timeline, but as we've all heard so many times, "Good things come to those who wait." But before you hunker down to wait for your trophy to walk out of the woods, you need to be prepared. You need to have a rifle that is sighted in so you know it will hit what you aim for. You need to have a comfortable seat so you don't have to repeatedly shift and reposition yourself. And you need to practice. I would have been far more successful at hunting if I had spent more time at target practice. But, if you are well-prepared and in position, you will be ready to act when the opportunity presents itself.

Today, look at your objectives and goals and determine what action you need to take right now so that you will be ready when the season for that opportunity opens for you. Look at your professional goals—what skills or certifications do you need to add to your resume to be ready to step into your next role? Take some steps today to get ready. Examine your personal life and your relationships. What can you do today to strengthen your marriage or help you be ready when the right person comes along?

Take action to become prepared and then, as you patiently work at being the best you can be, know that each day makes you more ready for the next great thing. Maybe you aren't there yet, but you're closer than you've ever been before!

CAPTIONS FOR LIFE

*"Captioning is the bridge to communication.
It is a visual tool that allows people to connect,
learn, and be entertained."*
Brenda Battat, former executive director, Hearing Loss
Association of America

Check the volume

"Wow! The TV is *loud*! Why?" I dramatically sign to my mother. She signs back while shrugging her shoulders, "Your sister's family was here yesterday." OK, that explains a lot! They crank the volume up so they can hear it over the other noises that accompany a visit. I've now been living on my own, away from my parents' home, for longer than the amount of time that I lived under their roof. That shift of location and focus have made some things very clear to me when I return to visit my parents. One of them is to always immediately check the volume when I turn on the TV at my Deaf parents' house.

Invariably, when my parents entertained visitors at their house, there was seldom agreement about the proper volume of the TV. So when I would turn it on, I'd find it was typically on one of two extremes of the spectrum—it was either on mute or set insanely high. If it was high, it was usually because their guests had watched a show with the TV set to a crazy high-volume level to drown out the other sounds in the room, or it was that one of my parents had inadvertently sat on the remote. Either way, the ear-splitting volume level was so high you could hear it from the thumb of Michigan all the way to the Upper Peninsula!

Regardless of where the volume level was set on the TV, there was always one constant factor, from as far back as I could remember—closed captions. We never watched any show without them. It was simply pointless in our household. My parents couldn't hear and therefore could not comprehend what was going on without the captions. And, I'd argue that watching shows with closed captioning helped me learn to read very quickly. If you wanted to read what was on the screen, you had to do it before the next group of words showed up.

But here's a slight curveball to close captioning that may surprise you. Today, in my own family's all-hearing household, we always have the captions visible when we watch TV. That's my preference for several reasons. It enables us to watch television at a quieter level, giving us the ability to talk while not missing what's happening on the screen. It also allows me to validate and clarify what I think I'm hearing on TV. And captions help me to stay focused on a show. I am easily distracted by things I hear, and if I am not relying on listening to the dialogue in the television show, I am less likely to have my attention pulled away from it.

The U.S. government also saw the benefit of closed captioning, and in 1980, it mandated that any screen 13 inches or larger must include a built-in closed-captioning decoder. During that time in history, televisions were already big and clunky and didn't need more bells and whistles added to them! They already weighed 300 pounds and occupied a huge chunk of your living room.

Accessibility matters

But closed captioning was important. It was one of the early improvements for Deaf people, giving them access to take advantage of the many services that televisions brought to their homes. Today, captions are readily available on all video monitors (as they should be). But the options that come with today's captions are miles ahead of where they were even a few years ago. I recently recognized this when I helped my mother set up her new television to stream various online program platforms. There is more to captions than just seeing the white letters over a black background. Now you have many font options. You can choose the color, size, and opacity of the words on your screen. Every platform that allows you to stream shows has its own menu of fonts, sizes, and colors that you can choose. None are the same. Several platforms still have some work to do. When you start to pay attention to the providers that offer accessibility tools, you quickly realize which platforms take accessibility seriously, doing it because they want to help their audience. You also see those who do it simply because it's a requirement.

I'm certain you know why accessibility is important. But humor me for a moment while I justify it. Deaf people rely on visual communication methods such as sign language and written language to communicate and receive information. Without accessibility tools, they face significant barriers to accessing important news, information, education, and job opportunities.

Accessibility matters for Deaf people because it helps remove barriers and promote inclusivity. It allows them to access information and entertainment, participate in cultural events, and reach their potential. Simply put, accessibility helps level the playing field with their hearing peers.

Next time when you are in a group setting and some attendees need accessibility, make sure you provide the most accessible environment possible. In the corporate world, recognize that accessibility is not a cost but a feature. It isn't the area where you want to curb funding to cut costs and increase profitability. Spend the money and make your product or service fully accessible...because accessibility really matters!

SOFTBALL WAS HIS EQUALIZER

"When a man steps up to the plate, we have
nothing but respect for him."
Eddie "The King" Feigner (King and His Court)

Diamonds were this man's best friend

Summertime in Michigan is beautiful. It's why
we put up with the long, cold winters! The long
days of almost perfect weather beckon us outside.
And that's where some of my best memories of my
father took place—outside in the summer, on the
softball diamond.

I was at his every game. I loved watching the
teamwork, the heckling of the players on the op-
posing team, and the high-fives among teammates
in the dugout. As a little kid, when I'd watch my
father stride up to the plate, taking his turn at bat,
reverence, and awe enveloped me.

My father was a great athlete in his prime. He
had a solid physique, and he funneled all that power
into his swing. More often than not, when he swung
at a pitch, two sounds followed—a loud ping as the
aluminum Louisville Slugger softball bat made solid

contact with the ball, and then the roar of the fans. Every game he came to play. He was totally in his element. He was made for this. Home plate with a bat in his hand was my father's domain. He was at home.

I don't recall seeing him ever lose a home run hitting contest. Besides being a power hitter, he played the two most important positions on the field: pitcher and catcher. On the mound, his modified knuckleball pitch had movement. It was sharp and then would fall—like dropping off a table—at a moment's notice.

As I grew older, my appreciation for the game of baseball grew. As a fan, I totally understood what my father brought to the game, and as an athlete, I envied him.

My father played competitive softball until I was approximately ten years old. He didn't stop playing because he had lost his edge. It was because I had been bitten by the baseball bug and was beginning to play competitively. My father decided it was my turn to play, and he gave up one of his great loves to help nurture my athletic dreams.

I can still recall every detail of those summer nights when he was playing. I would bring my baseball mitt and sprint to wherever there was a foul ball so I could retrieve it. You could see the gleam in his eyes as he would tell his teammates of his boy's growing abilities on the baseball field. During warmups, he would always step away to play catch with me. He would often pull me into the dugout to be the team's batboy or scorekeeper.

My dad's feats on the softball diamond were legendary.

My sister and I heard one story multiple times while we were growing up. It was even part of my Uncle Colt's eulogy at my father's funeral. The gist of the story is this: in my father's prime, he was part of a local team that played an exhibition game against a world-famous softball team called, "The King and His Court." Dressed in their trademark red, white, and blue uniforms, and taking the field as a four-man team—pitcher, catcher, first baseman, and shortstop—The King & His Court were America's premier family softball entertainment team, much like the Harlem Globetrotters were to basketball.

"The King" was Eddie Feigner, one of the greatest softball players of all time. Like my father, when he wasn't at bat, Eddie was pitching. He was an amazing pitcher. In fact, in 1967, Feigner appeared in a celebrity charity softball game against a group of Major League Baseball players. In that game, Feigner struck out Willie Mays, Willie McCovey, Brooks Robinson, Roberto Clemente, Maury Wills, and Harmon Killebrew...all in a row!

As the story goes, my father, the main character of my children's book, *Sky, the Deaf Home Run Hero,* stepped up to the plate, swung at a perfect pitch, and took "The King" deep! Batters rarely got a hit off Eddie Feigner, let alone did they take him deep for a home run. As I said, Feigner was an unbelievable pitcher. His career record is 141,517 strikeouts and 930 no-hitters. My father's home run that day ruined Eddie's potential no-hitter! Did I see it with my own eyes? No. But I've heard the story enough throughout my life from people I trust, and I've seen my father hit so many homers with my own eyes, that it only confirms to me his legendary status. So, I choose to believe it.

Hall of Famer Hank Aaron was one of the greatest hitters of all time. I think "The Hammer" would have liked my father. He once said, "In playing ball, and in life, a person occasionally gets the opportunity to do something great. When that time comes, only two things matter: being prepared to seize the moment and having the courage to take your best swing."

My father never lacked the courage to swing for the fence.

Although he was Deaf, there was no communication barrier for him on the softball diamond. His skill and results spoke for him. When I saw my father on the field and witnessed the way other players treated him, I realized that softball was his equalizer. On the diamond, his disability meant nothing. He cherished that time on the field, and in that venue, he wasn't different. He was treated like every other teammate—respected, loved, appreciated, and celebrated! He was equal.

What is your equalizer?

It didn't matter where the ball diamond was. In our neighborhood or hundreds of miles away, that's where my father felt at home. One of the definitions of an equalizer is something that makes things or people equal, putting them on a level playing field. Softball was my father's greatest equalizer, but his prowess as an athlete made almost any sport an equalizer for him.

Each of us has multiple equalizers that play a role in our lives. Equalizers help to bring context to our lives. There are many equalizers in our lives:

- Our connection with ourselves...how aware and present are you?
- Our health—mental, physical, spiritual...how do you care for the health of your mind, body, and spirit?
- Our relationships... how do you treat the ones you love?
- Our physical environment, home, car, office... how clean and orderly are those areas?
- Our wealth... how financially responsible are you?
- Our fulfillment as a person...how are you fulfilled every day?
- Our legacy... how are you contributing positively to your legacy every day?

Softball was my father's equalizer; he also excelled in many of these other areas. What is yours? The qualities I listed above can be equalizers for any of us.

Think about them and be honest with yourself. Where you are excelling and in which areas are you falling short? Those areas where you are doing well—keep going! For those that aren't quite as strong, decide to do some work in those areas.

Pick one of those weaker areas for you and start to improve it today. Don't pick all of them to fix at once. Start with one, and as you start to see progress, add another and another until you have leveled the playing field with those you might encounter in your life. Soon your equalizers will make room for you in your field of play—whether that's on an athletic field or a corporate boardroom.

The fact of the matter is that as humans, we are more alike than different. We should honor our diversity and individual differences, while simultaneously looking for the things that connect us—our similarities. In noticing and valuing our commonalities, we start seeing ourselves as equals and we find joy in our humanity.

Mark Twain is attributed with having written the following, "Twenty years from now you will be more disappointed by the things you didn't do than by the things you did. So throw off the bowlines. Sail away from the safe harbor... Explore. Dream."

Today, look for connections with the people around you. Seek out equalizers that unite you with them. Think about where you feel most "at home," and then build a group who can celebrate that feeling with you on your special "home plate."

HEY, BLUE!

"Any umpire who claims he has never missed a play is...
well, an umpire."
Ron Luciano, MLB umpire

Sports officiating is a thankless job

There's nothing like spending a beautiful summer's afternoon at a ballpark with your family and friends. The atmosphere is relaxed, and your peanuts and hotdog taste great as you cheer for your home team. Baseball is known as America's pastime for good reason—you're having a great time, and all seems right with the world.

Then the voice of some idiot rings out over the crowd, "Hey Ump, are you blind?"

Heckling the officials has become part of every sport, from the pros down to little league. It's as old as the game itself. We've probably all witnessed it—whether we were playing ball or watching from the stands—and we tolerate the abuse until it just gets too irritating. One fan always seems to take it too far. Knuckleheads like that can ruin a perfect day for everyone.

For more than thirty years, my father was an official. He loved team sports, and over the years he qualified to officiate baseball, softball, volleyball, basketball, and football games. What started as a side hustle—for him to make some extra money and stay close to the sports he loved—eventually turned into a fulfilling side job for him.

Dad started officiating as an umpire for softball and baseball games, wearing the familiar uniform with the blue shirt. His primary work position was directly behind the catcher, crouched down so he could be at eye level with the strike zone. This stance put his back facing the closest fans. Not surprisingly, the hecklers also liked to congregate in that area, near the batter, with a good view of the pitcher.

As a player, my father knew the strike zone very well and had a great eye for balls and strikes behind the plate. But sometimes the fans didn't agree with his call. That's when the knuckleheads would start hurling insults, "Hey Blue (referring to the color of the uniform shirt), Are you blind?" My father never flinched or reacted to their taunting and heckling.

The knuckleheads thought he was just ignoring them, which made them get even more loud and boisterous. They had no idea he was Deaf and couldn't hear a word they were saying.

To most of the fans who were out to enjoy a nice game, the yelling was just an irritation, but to my sister and me, hearing the ridicule was infuriating.

We tried ignoring it, but after years of sucking it up, we finally couldn't take it anymore, and we'd snap back at the knuckleheads in defense of our father.

But our dad didn't need to be defended. He was in full control. He knew exactly what was going on around him at all times. He knew who was pushing the limits, and in basketball, he knew when to call a "T" (technical foul) and eject someone. After those games, we'd talk about what happened, and my sister and I would tell him what we heard. He'd just shake his head and tell us not to worry about it. Often, he'd show a slight smile and call the person a name I'm choosing not to repeat.

Officiating was one of my father's "equalizers." It gave him a position of equality in the hearing world. I'll never forget the pride he demonstrated when he was officially recognized for having reached the huge milestone of twenty years of officiating for the Michigan High School Athletic Association (MHSAA). He continued to officiate for thirteen more years after that for a total of thirty-three years. He was proud of being an official and wearing the uniform. In fact, the last picture we have of him, taken two days before his death, is a photo of my father in his full umpiring gear at the last game he would ever call as an official.

I respected my father as a man, and I respected him as an official. He enters my mind every time I'm at a game and see an official in action. That's why—even though I may disagree vehemently with a call—you'll never see me be a rude knucklehead. I've experienced first-hand how nasty and spiteful it can become, and it's one of the very few things I dislike in organized athletics.

I have always admired the backbone of anyone who has the guts to get out on the field and make the hard calls. We need more people who are willing to blow the whistle even when they know it won't be popular with the home crowd. And it's way past time for them to receive honor and respect for doing it.

Don't be a knucklehead

We have all encountered knuckleheads and hecklers in life. They pop up almost everywhere and make any job more difficult than it has to be. But if your love of sports leads you down the track of officiating, you will likely encounter more knuckleheads than most. Sadly, some 80 percent of all new high school athletic officials quit within two years, primarily because of the abuse they receive from out-of-control fans.

My sister and I would try to figure out why some people in the stands could quietly disagree with a call and boo or shake their head, but others would cross the line and become mean, hurtful, and demeaning. How could people do this to another human being? I discovered several factors. Knuckleheads often lack self-awareness and empathy for others. They tend to react quickly, be impulsive, and don't take responsibility for their actions, even while they hold others to a high standard of behavior.

You don't want to be a knucklehead. Nobody wants to be that person. Look at their actions and learn from them, not as a role model but as an example of how not to act.

Today, wherever you are and whatever you find yourself doing, be aware of your words and actions and how they impact the people around you. Put yourself in their shoes and think about how your actions might be interpreted by them. Slow down and take time to think about what you're about to do or say, and consider the potential consequences. Even then, you'll sometimes mess up. It's probably not the end of the world. Admit what you did, own up to your mistakes, take responsibility for your actions, make it right, and then start working to improve in that area of your life.

So today, look around. Do you see any knuckleheads in the cheap seats waiting for the first opportunity to pounce on you and humiliate you when you mess up? Be proactive, think before you act or speak, and take them out of the game in your head. Don't let their criticism slow you down or discourage you from doing the job you came to do.

And as you look around, notice how people are reacting to you. Could you be acting like a knucklehead in their lives? Are you exhibiting any of those behaviors? If so, knock it off! You can be better than that!

Don't be a knucklehead in the game of life.

TOILET PAPER, EGGS, AND UNDERWEAR

*"Good humor is a tonic for mind and body. It
is the best antidote for anxiety and depression.
It is a business asset. It attracts and keeps friends.
It lightens human burdens."*
Grenville Kleiser, author and professor

The Chase

Kids will be kids, and often pulling pranks and acting foolish is part of going through that odd phase of adolescence. Toilet-papering and egging a classmate's house are a couple of those pranks that have been around for many years. Well, at least until the COVID-19 pandemic hit, and then overnight, toilet paper turned into a precious commodity (except for that crappy single-ply stuff that we all have sworn we will never buy again).

TPing and egging are pranks mostly carried out by high schoolers, which is when I experienced them. I was often on the receiving end and felt these pranks were a type of bullying. I hated them, not just because I felt targeted, but also because they created extra work for me. My father felt these must be my friends who were doing this, so whenever it happened, I was expected to clean it all up. Picking up broken eggshells, pulling toilet paper out of trees, and hosing down the yard wasn't the way I wanted to spend my time after school.

I looked at it as a degrading waste of my time, but my father took those pranks as a personal insult. He saw them as attacks and blatant acts of disrespect perpetrated by young undisciplined brats. It was just eggs and toilet paper, but he felt that these kids were damaging his family's home. And that was just too much to ignore.

It was a fall Saturday night, one of those perfect Michigan weekends when the air was crisp, the sky brilliant blue, and the leaves were turning blazing shades of red, yellow, and orange. All should be nice and peaceful on a Saturday evening like this, but my father was far from relaxed. He was on high alert. The previous weekend, our house had been TPed and egged, and my father wanted to catch those scoundrels in the act—if they dared show up again.

Our home had a big window that looked out of the living room onto the front yard. It was a perfect vantage point, with a full view of our 30-foot pine tree which was the frequent target of the TP bandits. Most evenings, my parents would close the blinds on the front window to provide more privacy for us in the house, but since my father was in full security guard mode, he left just enough of the blinds open so he could position himself at the window, hidden from view from the street, but able to keep an eye on the yard.

My sister and I went to bed, followed by our mother. Dad stayed at his post by the window. *Saturday Night Live* was on the TV, and he was about to doze off when he noticed movement in the front yard. He strained to get a better look just as the first roll of toilet paper came flying through the air toward our big pine tree.

The leg rest on his recliner slammed down, as he jumped out of the chair. He flipped on the outside lights and sprinted out the door into the front yard, wearing only a white undershirt and tighty-whities. He was in hot pursuit, fueled by rage and determined to defend his castle. Loud unintelligible noises spewed out of his mouth, as he waved his arms and ran directly toward the kids who were armed with multiple rolls of toilet paper.

Those kids feared for their lives. They thought this was a night of harmless fun, but now they were scrambling in all directions to keep away from this seemingly deranged five-foot-eleven-inch, 220-pound man sprinting toward them, wearing tighty-whities.

Hearing the noise and ruckus in the front yard, I came out of my bedroom to get the update. Slightly out of breath, my father came back into the house and signed, "I know who did it. That kid is a jerk."

That was the last time our home was TPed or egged. Word traveled quickly at school that Mickey's dad was not someone to mess with.

Jokes > Pranks

I am certain that the kids caught in the act at our house were not expecting to get chased by a crazed tighty-whitie Grim Reaper. It had an indelible impact on them and me. They understood that if they feared death, they should stay away from Mickey's house. And I realized that jokes were mightier than pranks, an idea that stuck with me throughout my life.

Jokes and pranks are two very different forms of humor. Jokes typically involve a punchline that is meant to make *other* people laugh—like my dad jokes. They are usually harmless and don't cause damage to others. Jokes can be shared among friends or in a social setting, and they are meant to make people feel good.

On the other hand, pranks are often physical and involve tricking or fooling someone for your own amusement. While most pranks may be intended as harmless and fun, others can cause harm, damage property, or problems for others. Pranks can also be seen as a form of bullying or disrespect, and in some cases, they can be illegal.

When compared to pranks, I think that jokes tend to be a safer and more universally appreciated form of humor. Jokes are easier to control and can be tailored to the audience, whereas pranks are often unpredictable, can easily get out of hand, and may not be well-received by those on the receiving end.

My point isn't to convince you that jokes are a better form of humor. I'll let you decide for yourself. Here's what I would like you to do...

Today, think about lightening the mood around you. If you notice a coworker or a family member is finding it hard to smile, bring some levity to the moment. Tell a joke or play a prank that makes you look foolish—help them laugh!

Life is meant to have some humor in it. To my Deaf friends, keep telling the classic Deaf jokes such as "The Hotel," "The Timberman," and "The Hitchhiker." To the dads reading this, keep telling those corny dad jokes. Your kids probably won't laugh out loud, but they'll smile...or at least groan! When you want to bring humor into a situation, especially at work, do it in a way that respects others. Don't play pranks on people. You've hopefully outgrown that by now anyhow.

Remember, if your attempt at humor makes someone angry, there might be a big, crazy, barrel-chested guy running at you to teach you a lesson... wearing tighty-whities! And trust me, you don't want to see that. You will thank me for it later.

Mom Dad Not Hear

A CODA WITHOUT A NAME SIGN

"The world would be a better place if doctors were
less enthusiastic about fixing Deaf people."
Dr. Candace McCullough, founder,
Deaf Counseling Center

What's your name sign?

As an adult CODA, my first interaction with new acquaintances in any Deaf support group would always include introductions using American Sign Language. I would spell out my name using hand symbols for the letters M-I-C-K-E-Y. They would smile and pause, waiting for my next move. Then they would ask me for my name sign.[6] I'd shrug and tell them I didn't have one. Then I'd get an odd, quizzical look in return. I knew what that look meant. My CODA credibility was being questioned.

I'm a Child of Deaf Adults (CODA), and I don't have a name sign. I'm an exception to the rule. People born into Deaf families usually are given a unique name sign. My sister has one, but I don't. Although it is highly unusual, for some reason I don't recall ever wondering as a kid why I didn't have a name sign.

The topic came up recently when I was introduced to the board of directors for the Deaf and Hard of Hearing Services. On the east side of the state, in the tight-knit Deaf community where I grew up, everyone knew who Mickey was, and I knew who they were. But a new Deaf community can be protective and skeptical when considering welcoming someone new. Not having a name sign was so unusual that it was the equivalent of a red flag to these new acquaintances.

In Deaf culture, a name sign is a unique sign used to identify a particular person. It is a form of personal identification, much like a logo or a written signature. A name sign can only be given to a person by someone else within the Deaf community. You cannot create a name sign for yourself. Typically, name signs are based on a person's physical or personality traits, hobbies, or other distinctive characteristics.

I asked my mother recently why I didn't have a name sign. She said it was due in part to the fact that she never had a name sign. That was a casualty from her youth. Kids can be cruel, and as a child, it was pointed out to her that the initials of her name were B and J—a two-letter abbreviation that often has a sexual connotation. She didn't want to be joked about in that way, so she opted out of having a name sign, and her friends would just spell out her first name using finger signs instead: B-O-N-N-I-E. She told me that she and my dad never thought it was a priority for me to have a name sign, since I wasn't Deaf. So it never happened.

In case you're wondering, my sister's name sign is a "T," while making the sign of a baby with it, and my father's name sign was a big "S" sign, traced on your chest like Superman. For him, that was appropriate.

Despite not having a name sign, I never once felt as if I wasn't included or connected to the Deaf community as I was growing up.

Inclusion matters

I know some people feel that diversity, equity, and inclusion (DE&I) have become divisive buzzwords in our culture today. And I understand that, but as a society, we need to get intentional about those things, because we still have a long way to go before those on the fringes feel accepted by general society. If you ask people close to the Deaf community, they will say that we should also add to DE&I the word "Accessibility"—and I agree with them.

Inclusion is still a big issue for Deaf adults and children. Name signs serve as an important aspect of Deaf culture and a way for Deaf individuals to establish their identity and feel a sense of belonging within their community.

Having a name sign means that someone has been accepted, that a Deaf person felt close enough to them to honor them with their own unique brand. But that isn't the only benefit of a name sign. In the "Deaf blunt" communication style, they are a quick and efficient way of identifying a particular individual, and as such they help break down communication barriers.

Another great thing about name signs is the ability for a hearing person to show their respect and acceptance of Deaf people by learning and using their name sign. This enables a greater understanding of Deaf people within the broader community. This impact can help their involvement in general society and reduce their feelings of isolation and loneliness.

Having a name sign can also be an important tool for enhancing the social and cultural experiences of Deaf people. By recognizing and respecting the unique aspects of Deaf culture, we can create a more inclusive and accepting society for everyone.

Look at yourself. Are you an inclusive person? Do you make it a point to respect and include everyone, regardless of how different they may seem to be compared to you and your circle of friends? If not, take this as a nudge today, a push towards being more intentional about inclusion in all facets of your life.

LESSONS FROM PART TWO
LIFE

1 You can make a great first impression by learning people's names and pronouncing them correctly. When you meet someone new, listen carefully to hear how they pronounce their name, and then remember it to use the next time you see them.

2 Life brings certain unplanned—and often unwanted—events for a reason. Through them, you can learn grit and how to work through hardships. Adversity can help shape you into a better person. Three lessons I learned the hard way: don't make life decisions based on emotions, being humbled makes you work harder, and don't quit if you hit a roadblock. Just keep going.

3 Be honest about your own strengths and weaknesses. Don't try to save money by doing something you don't know how to do. Know your skillset and be ready to reach out to a professional when you need one. It will save you time, headaches, and money in the long run!

4 It's never too late to start learning something new. Maybe it's another language or a different way of communicating. Grow your gray matter and stretch your capacity to learn and relate to people who are different from you. Your world will be enriched as a result.

5 Get prepared and be patient. Then you'll be in position and ready to take action when the opportunity presents itself. Examine your objectives and goals and determine what action you need to take to be ready when the season for that opportunity opens for you.

6 Make accessibility a priority in your life. Keep your eyes open for ways that you can help level the playing field for those who need it. Recognize that accessibility is not a cost but a feature—in every area of life. Do not exclude people if you have the ability to make them feel welcome.

7 Think about where you are excelling, and where you're falling short. Strengthen those areas where you are doing well, and make connections to share them with like-minded people. For those areas that aren't quite as strong, decide to work on them. Try new things. Build your weaknesses as well as your strengths, and don't be afraid to get out there and get in the game!

8 **Expect criticism, especially when you've messed up.** Admit what you did, own up to your mistakes, take responsibility for your actions, make it right, and then start working to improve in that area of your life. Be careful not to criticize others. Think before you act or speak, and don't let other people's opinions slow you down.

9 **When it comes to humor, jokes are better and safer than pranks.** Jokes are meant to make people feel good, while pranks often make their target feel bad, bullied, or disrespected. When you make someone laugh, don't let it be at someone's expense.

10 **People want to feel accepted.** By recognizing and respecting the unique aspects of the people you interact with, you can create a more inclusive and accepting society for everyone. Make it a point to respect and include everyone, regardless of how different they may seem to be compared to you and your circle of friends.

.

PART THREE

LOVE

Mom Dad Not Hear

HOW DID YOU LEARN SIGN LANGUAGE?

"Language is, quite literally, the stuff of life. The more you can speak of other people's languages, the more you can be part of their lives and enrich your own."
Paddy Ashdown, politician and diplomat

It's the wrong question

Most of the people I meet speak English, and it's the only language they have ever spoken fluently. Of course, many have studied French, Spanish, or German in high school, and they realize just how hard it can be to gain fluency in a language that is not your mother tongue. So, when people ask me how I learned sign language, they are assuming that I grew up hearing English being spoken at home—that sign language must have been my second language. Wrong. They should be asking me, "How did you learn English?"

My first language was American Sign Language (ASL). My mother didn't sing me to sleep or read books to me in English like most American babies hear every day. I wasn't speaking, but I found ways to communicate—typically by pinching and pointing.

I got my point across like many infants and toddlers do, but unlike most kids, my growth into using vocal speech had a bit of a lag.

I don't recall many of the specifics, but I do remember working with a speech therapist when I was in elementary school. There were a few problems I needed to overcome. Not only was I not hearing English being spoken at home, but it was also effectively my second language, and added on top of that was the physical impact of being born with a cleft lip and a cleft palate. It was hard. As a kid, I struggled to communicate and fit in with my classmates.

Not long ago, my mother and I were talking about that season of my life, and she revealed that she and my dad tried to be very intentional about exposing my sister and me to the hearing world. They would take us to visit extended family, enrolled us at daycare so we could make friends with speaking kids, and signed us up for many extracurricular activities. While Mom acknowledged that it was a lot of work, in my parents' mind, it was imperative to create these learning environments for us. And I'm so glad they did, but it was still difficult.

ASL is efficient

In addition to lagging behind in physically being able to speak, it took me even longer to become comfortable using the English language. By its nature, American Sign Language is a fast, straight-to-the-point, and concise language. ASL has two ways to communicate a word. The basic way is finger spelling, where you spell out the word letter-by-letter using hand shapes. The other way uses one sign for an entire word or phrase. That's the method Deaf people prefer.

The culture of ASL is to be as specific as possible and use as few words as you can to convey a message. For instance, here are two examples showing the differences in ASL versus spoken English communication:

Telling someone your parents are Deaf:

English: "My mother and father are Deaf."

ASL: Three signs—Mother, Father, Deaf.

Telling someone you love them:

English: "I Love You."

ASL: One sign.

The best results come from communicating in your native tongue

Nelson Mandela said, "If you speak to a man in a language he understands, that goes to his head. If you speak to him in his own language, that goes to his heart."

I have seen Mandela's point play out in multiple situations. Recently, I was at a local restaurant having dinner with my mother. Our young waitress realized she was Deaf and asked me, "Can I try signing with her?" I smiled and replied, "Sure, go ahead. She loves it."

The young lady didn't know much sign language, but she succeeded in saying a few things. My mother was thrilled. It meant so much to her that someone would attempt to talk to her in her own language. She isn't known for being a big tipper, but that day, my mother tipped the young lady well, all because she tried.

The same thing happens in business. Fortunately for most Americans, globalization has made English the business language of the world. However, that does not mean it is the most effective way to talk with business partners internationally. My team and I regularly communicate across continents and languages. When we find that we are struggling to get resolutions or engagement via English, we tap into Google Translate to convert our message to their native language. And even though the translation is sometimes far from perfect, like the young waitress discovered, even a basic attempt at using a person's native language is appreciated. And wouldn't you know it, we often get answers far more quickly than if we had stubbornly insisted on using English!

Today, if you encounter someone who has English as a second language, make an effort to meet them in their world. Try at least a greeting. You'll show them honor and make them smile! Don't be afraid of sounding foolish. Focus on the person you're talking to—and try speaking to their heart and not just their head.

Mom Dad Not Hear

THE DEAF CLUB

*"At home, I'm the only deaf person. When I'm here,
I can communicate."*
Álex Garcia, actor

A place where everybody knew my name

If it was Saturday night, our family would be found at 3520 Schust Road: The Deaf Club. The place would be filled with happy people and far too much smoke! But contrary to popular belief, it wasn't quiet. I can still visualize the details of the building to this very day, and it's been over twenty years since I've spent time in the place.

Outside, it had a façade of yellow brick and a walkway leading to an entryway with double glass doors that swung outward. If you walked straight in, you'd find yourself in the bar area, complete with a television, darts, shuffleboard, and a jukebox. Why they installed a jukebox always seemed a bit odd to me. From the bar, turn left, and a long hallway would take you to the kitchen, restrooms, and an event space where theme parties and card nights would take place. Also, down that hallway was the game room where I'd spend all my quarters playing my favorite arcade game: *Galaga*.

That place is to blame for my sister and me entering the world! It's the Tri-City Association for the Deaf, located in Saginaw, Michigan—affectionately known as "The Deaf Club." My mother and father met here during a New Year's Eve Party in 1980. They were engaged by Valentine's Day and married in October. Their favorite child showed up in July of the following year, and my sister came along a couple of years later.

The Deaf Club was their community. It was their tribe. These were the people our parents socialized with, so my sister and I ended up being there quite a lot, hanging out with other CODAs (Child of Deaf Adults). What was cool was how we were treated. The club seemed to look for reasons to celebrate with each of the CODAs. When you made the honor roll, they honored you. If you were on a sports team, they'd make your athletic feats sound legendary. In that building, if you were a CODA, you were one of them, you belonged, and every single Deaf person embraced you. Who wouldn't love a community that made you feel so special and celebrated?

Community is everything

Having a close community where you feel welcomed and safe, where you fit in, is critical to everyone's well-being, and the Deaf Club was the first place I learned about true community. As in every community, drama invariably happens. But what I saw in the Deaf Club was how the members of that community quickly shifted from any internal discord back into harmony. They seemed to innately understand the well-known quote from the Greek storyteller, Aesop, "United we stand, divided we fall."

This was their community, and they had each other's backs. The only people allowed to cause strife within that community were the members themselves, and any conflict was quickly resolved. But if there was any disturbance from the outside world, the members would defend their tribe with levels of camaraderie you rarely see demonstrated anywhere else.

Participating in a community bonded by shared attitudes, values, and goals is an essential ingredient to enjoying a fulfilling life. The absence of social connections can have profound effects on our overall health, including higher levels of stress and inflammation, chronic disease, and even mental illness. Strong social ties help people thrive. Ultimately, being part of a supportive community will enable you to better cope with difficult challenges, give you help in solving problems, and celebrate your life's successes.

If you're already part of such a community, it is something to be thankful for. But if you're looking for your tribe, I caution you to be selective. The community that is meant for you is the one that inspires you, gives you strength, defends you, and holds you and its other members accountable to be the best version of themselves.

Seek out the people who have enough capacity for you in their lives and are not already over-committed. Look for the people who need you—not just the people you want to hang out with or think you can profit from. As you form a community that truly cares about its members, resolves disputes quickly, and defends its own against outside threats, look to give more than you receive. Today, find time to connect with your community and let them know how much they mean to you.

DOCTOR VISITS THEN AND NOW

"Accessibility allows us to tap into everyone's potential."
Debra Ruh, advocate and entrepreneur

Then and Now

On July 26, 1990, President George H.W. Bush signed into law the "Americans with Disabilities Act" (ADA), the most sweeping affirmation of rights for people with disabilities in American history to that time. My mother remembers it well. She was 36 years of age when the ADA was signed into law, and up until then, she had been living in a civil rights struggle her entire life.

Until recently, I understood the "now," but I didn't understand the "then." So, I asked my mother to explain to me what doctor visits were like for her before the passing of the ADA since this legislation helped to enforce the hiring of professional sign language interpreters at medical facilities. Here's my conversation with my mom:

Q: How did you make a doctor's appointment back then?

A: If I was at the doctor's office, and I needed a follow-up visit, I would make the appointment while I was still right there at the doctor's office. If I needed to see a doctor for an initial visit, I would use our teletypewriter (TTY) to call the Michigan Relay Service and ask them to telephone the doctor's office for me. Or I would just ask you to call for me!

Q: Did you have qualified, professional interpreters on your visits?

A: No, back then if I wanted a professional, I had to pay for them out of my own pocket. That wasn't feasible, and I felt I was probably able to manage the communication well enough myself. If I needed an adult to accompany me, I would bring my mom (your grandmother) with me. I never asked you to interpret at my doctors' visits. You were a young boy, and that was too personal. You were too young at that time.

Q: How did you communicate with the nurses and doctors?

A: I had a notebook, where I kept my current medications written down at all times. The medical staff and I would typically write back and forth to each other on the back of the visit notes.

Q: Did you start getting interpreters right away when ADA was put into law?

A: No, we lived in a small place, and businesses did not adopt the law right away. It took a lot of advocacy and energy for many years to ensure that companies would abide by ADA laws. It still happens today, but we are more informed about how to address it.

Q: What about times when you needed surgery? Who was in the room typically?

A: Early on, it was always your grandmother and your father. It was both of them because your father was my life partner and since my mother could hear, she could be my voice and advocate. But after ADA was in place, at times I would have a certified interpreter provided to be with me at the hospital.

After this conversation, I'm still in awe at how different life was for my parents just a few decades ago. If I hadn't asked my mother those questions, I would have taken for granted the accessibility she now has. Many things have changed, yet some things have stayed the same.

After our father passed away in 2021 at the age of sixty-five, my sister and I watched as mom tried to arrange for her own increasing medical needs in our hometown area. My sister and I were not able to be at every one of her appointments, and sadly my mom's diabetes was getting worse.

We had many difficult discussions as a family, eventually deciding that all of our mother's medical care should be moved to West Michigan, where she could be sure her healthcare providers were the best. We knew we had to make an immediate course correction. If her diabetes progressed further, we risked having both a Deaf and Blind mother.

While the West Michigan healthcare system certainly deserves its accolades, it isn't without flaws. I was reminded of that while accompanying Mom to one of her appointments.

Normally, if there is a professional interpreter scheduled to work, they will meet us in the waiting room lobby. On this day, there wasn't one. We waited and waited for someone to show up, but they never did. Mom and I looked at one another and shrugged. We've been in this situation before. She knew I would interpret if needed.

We were brought down the hall into the procedure room. As the nurse and doctor walked in, I asked where the interpreter was. They held up an iPad with pride, "We are going to call them now." To their credit, they weren't doing anything against the law. They were using technology to provide access to a translator.

At that moment in time, I had a choice to make. A choice many CODAs have experienced in similar situations. Option One: save time and just tell the doctor that this solution is not going to work. Option Two: let it play out and see the "ah-ha" moment when they realize on their own that it is not going to work. Based on my read of the doctor in that short window of time, I decided to go with Option Two.

They dialed the number to the Video Relay Interpreter (VRI), and up popped a live person on the other end, ready to relay the words the doctor was speaking. My mother was there at an appointment with an eye doctor for a reason. She could not see well. She asked the nurse to hold the 10.9-inch iPad closer and closer until it was four inches from her face, where my frustrated mother signed, "Can't see." I looked at the doctor and nurse and told them that I would take over interpreting. We thanked the interpreter and ended the call.

After the procedure was completed and the nurse cleaned up, I confirmed what they now understood—my mother needs to have an in-person interpreter at all appointments going forward. Having been in situations like this many times before, I realized it was an opportunity to educate. While a Video Relay Interpreter (VRI) is legally acceptable, common sense should be used and patient preference should be taken into consideration. In this situation, the doctor's office overestimated the ability of a patient with low vision to clearly see and interact with the interpreter on the screen. Deaf people rely so heavily on their vision for communication that it is the responsibility of the provider to clearly communicate the medical treatment plan to the patient using the most effective means possible.

Without a doubt, doctors' visits are much more accessible than they used to be in the earlier periods of my parents' lives. But there is always a need for improvement and advocacy.

Be a great advocate

I admit that empathy has never been my forte. Typically, I lean more toward a no-nonsense business mindset. That is how my mind works. But after my father passed away, I started advocating for my mother. Looking back, I must have always had that ability within me, but now I'm seeing myself grow in that area. I truly love my mother, and I want to make sure she has what she needs. I'm not the little kid anymore who was limited to answering the phone and helping her with errands. Now I'm an adult who has gained some wisdom and knows at this point in life how to make things happen.

People will often advise you to be your own advocate in many settings. I've been told that throughout life—in my career while getting my education, and when negotiating things for my family. That advice is all well and good, as long as you are advocating within the same communication realm as the other people involved. But what if you are trying to advocate for yourself, and you are faced with the great disadvantage of not even being able to communicate in the same language? You're doing your best, but the situation may require more. That is when other capable people are needed to step in to aid and assist you—to be your advocate.

These amazing people exist! I have seen some great advocates for the Deaf community in my life. It is remarkable to see a well-educated advocate take on someone who isn't providing access to the community. If you've ever seen a trial lawyer slice up a witness in a court of law, it can be very similar, the stuff movies are made of!

What I have learned in life is the necessity to advocate strongly, for yourself and those you love, but also for those who need the help you have the talent to provide. Look at your life and those around you. First, are you advocating well for yourself? If not, make some changes and start standing up for yourself today. Secondly, are you successfully advocating for the people you love and care about? If not, you need to step up and do more. These people depend on you. If you truly love and care about them, you will also care for them and advocate for them. Thirdly, are there people on your work team who need an advocate—perhaps because English is not their first language or because of a learning disability or other qualities that hold them back and push them down? You can be the bridge that sets them on the path to success. It all starts with becoming a person who exhibits empathy. Plug into that superpower today! Somebody close to you needs an advocate. They need *you*.

Mom Dad Not Hear

THE EVOLUTION OF CALLING THE CAROLANS

*"The telephone is an instrument of communication,
not a means of seduction."*
Fran Lebowitz, author and speaker

Ring, flash, and a beep

I grew up in the days before everyone had their own cell phone. Back then, every home had one phone line (called a landline) which was hard-wired to the phone company. When the phone would ring, there would be a real person who wanted to speak with someone in the home. Every family had its own scenario that played out when the telephone rang. Often, in a home with a teenager, that's who would yell out, "I've got it," as they would run to answer the phone.

In our house growing up, things were a bit different. When the phone rang, my sister and I were the only ones who could hear it. A moment later, a light would flash in several of the rooms of the house to let my mother and father know that a call was coming in. If my sister or I were home, then one of us would normally answer, "Hello?"

If we didn't hear the caller's voice, we waited. We were taught to never hang up if it seemed like nobody was there. Usually, after a short wait, we'd begin to hear beeping tones, like a Morse code sound. That was the signal telling us that we needed to place the handset of the phone on top of the TTY (teletypewriter) receiver. We would sit in front of the machine, which looked like an ancient desktop computer, and we would type, "Hello this is Mickey, GA" (GA stands for Go Ahead). Then the person on the other end of the line would respond, and my mother or father would sit down at the TTY keyboard and take over the conversation.

Being patient and waiting to hear a voice or electronic signal on the other end of the phone was crucial. Sometimes we didn't have enough patience. If we listened to nothing but silence for too long, we'd give up and hang up the phone. As soon as we had walked away from the phone—without fail—it would ring again. This time we would wait as long as it took to hear several beeps from the caller's TTY, telling us to connect the machine on our end for our parents.

The TTY was a staple in our house from the time my parents were married until the mid-2000s. That's when technology started giving everyone— Deaf people included—many more communication options. Internet use was widespread, and Video Relay Services (VRS) began to take over as the primary mode of communication. In the mid-2000s, my parents gave up their trusty but antiquated TTY and joined the VRS bandwagon.

VRS is a much more straightforward and user-friendly communication system. You still hear the ring, followed by a flashing light of the incoming call, but there is no more waiting for the beep and connecting the phone to a machine. With VRS, you either have the opportunity to call from one Deaf person to another and chat using American Sign Language, or you have the opportunity to use the relay service provided, where the Deaf person communicates with an interpreter on the screen who is speaking verbally to the hearing person on the other end of the phone.

Today, my mother and I just use our cell phones and a video messenger app. There are several other options, but we've found a platform that my mother understands and is easy for her to use, so we stick with it.

Video calling was a game changer when communicating with my parents. They got to see their children's faces, and most importantly, they could visually communicate with their grandchildren. The TTY was impersonal, but video chats were totally personal.

In fact, in the six months prior to my father's death, he would video call us nearly every night and have a blast talking with his 1½-year-old grandson and his 4½-year-old granddaughter. My father and son would compete to see who could be the funniest and flash the biggest smile. Those are precious memories.

I'm grateful for the evolution in the technology that allows Deaf people to communicate with each other, as well as with their hearing friends and family members. Video has made it much more personable and real than the type of conversations that took place via the TTY.

Technological innovation can be great

I believe many of us would agree that we have a love/hate relationship with new technology. We've seen it used for both good and evil over our lifetimes.

When it comes to communication, technology has revolutionized how we interact with each other. This has impacted everyone, and Deaf people and their families have benefited greatly. I think there are a few lessons we can all glean from the huge changes in the ways Deaf people have communicated electronically over the past thirty or so years.

First, the TTY taught me that patience and understanding are important. That technology required a specific protocol, and hanging up too soon would result in missed communication. Sometimes those messages were important. The evolution of technology has made communication easier and more accessible, but it is still critical to be patient and understanding, both of the other person on the line and the age and agility of the technological tool we are using.

Second, we should be happy when technology works, and celebrate when it evolves and gives us improved service. The transition from the TTY to VRS was a revolutionary shift in communication options for the Deaf community. The improvement of the quality, accessibility, and options for visual and audible communication it gave people like my parents was paradigm shifting.

Third, technological innovations have helped on-line communication finally feel personal and real. The ability for Deaf people to make a video call and see the faces of the people they are communicating with has made a significant difference in their enjoyment and satisfaction with the experience. Across continents and time zones, technology continues to bring people together faster and better than ever before and helps them stay in touch with family and friends.

Finally, technology has helped remove barriers to effective communication. Video calls have made it possible for Deaf people to communicate more easily with hearing friends and relatives, and for hearing individuals to have more options in communicating with Deaf people. Language has always been a huge barrier to effective communication. Today countless translation apps enable individuals and organizations to communicate cross-culturally.

Today, if you're facing communication barriers with someone, don't settle for just not speaking. Look for a solution to remove the barrier. It may be a technological solution, but it might just require patience and spending time to be sure that your message and your concern for the person is getting through. Don't let yourself get frustrated and give up. Instead, pursue finding a solution. Keep an open mind, and whether it's a new technology that provides the key, or spending the time that interpersonal communication requires, embrace the solution and celebrate the breakthroughs. Anything that improves the quality of your communication—especially with family and friends—should certainly be taken seriously.

SON, DAUGHTER DEAF

"Early intervention, including access to language and communication, is crucial for the development of deaf and hard of hearing children."
American Society for Deaf Children

A tale of two languages

If you are born Deaf, 90% of the time, your parents have normal hearing. That was the case for both of my parents. My mother was born to Walter and Meta, and my father was born to Joseph and Irene. All four of them could hear, but only one learned sign language well enough to communicate with their child. That was my grandmother Meta.

For years I've wondered why a parent wouldn't work to learn the only language that their child could use to communicate. I still don't fully understand it, but I cut them some slack. It was a different time in society and each family had their unique dynamics.

For example, my mother spent every school year at the Michigan School for the Deaf, a boarding school in Flint, Michigan. Every Monday she would travel fifty minutes to begin the school week. Then every Friday, it would be another fifty minutes from

Flint back home to Caro. Sometimes she would ride in a car but other times she'd have to take a public bus. Once that bus dropped her off in Bay City, in the 1960s when there were no cell phones, only pay phones, and she was Deaf.

Initially, the school administrators advised my grandparents not to use sign language with my mother at home to strengthen her oral communication and lip reading. That advice changed once the school realized that despite the demands and intentions of the Deaf education experts, the students were going to continue to communicate using ASL as their primary language. That's when my grandmother began to learn. I have nothing but respect for her grit and determination to learn how to sign back in the 1960s when there was very little access to any training materials. Learning a language is still hard work for most of us, but today we have so many online tools and excellent books and courses for any language, including ASL.

My father, on the other hand, grew up in a traditional school without exposure to sign language or access to training in American Sign Language. In fact, he had to teach himself. His family and school system didn't have many resources to help him, so he didn't have the access to specialized training that a young Deaf child needed.

His father was gone, and he was raised by a stepfather. His mother, trying to juggle all of the stuff life threw at her, never really grasped sign language. I recall many times while growing up watching my dad and grandmother trying to communicate. It was painful. There was absolutely zero conversation that was of any value between them. Neither one of them understood the other, and before long, they would both get frustrated and just give up. I know my father was envious that my mother was able to communicate well with her mother. My dad never had that with either of his parents.

So why did three of my four grandparents struggle to learn sign language well enough to talk to their kids? I've wrestled with this unanswerable question for so long. The best I can come up with is simply that it was a combination of reasons. Learning a new language requires a huge time commitment, and that takes dedication. When I became a parent, I discovered that it isn't always easy to understand what a child is saying, especially when the child is just learning the language. Since sign language uses a significant amount of body language and gestures, it can be difficult to determine if a child is trying to communicate or just being active, as kids do. And, of course, the lack of easy access to good training materials made learning ASL much harder than it should have been for parents of Deaf children.

These are some of the many reasons why I cut my grandparents some slack. I know it was difficult for them to learn ASL, but I still don't want to let them off the hook entirely. I fully believe that parents and their kids need to be able to communicate—deeply—about things that matter to them. Parents are the ones in charge; they can make decisions about how they will use their time and determine what is important to do. One of those decisions should be to learn sign language well enough to be able to communicate easily with their Deaf child.

Deaf children should be fluent in American Sign Language

The amount of technology available to provide better accessibility for Deaf children has caused some people to drift away from achieving ASL fluency. Many parents have decided to get cochlear implants for their Deaf children and use English as their primary language. However, research data strongly supports the importance of providing Deaf and Hard of Hearing children with access to sign language very early as their primary language.[7]

There are four key reasons that parents of deaf children should communicate in sign language: language development, socialization, academic success, and cognitive development. When there is a deficiency in any one of those four areas, there tends to be a corresponding negative impact as these children progress from childhood to adolescence and into adulthood.

Studies have shown that deaf children who are exposed to ASL early in life tend to have better overall language development and comprehension than those who are not.[8] This is because ASL is a fully formed and complete language with its own syntax and grammar, and it allows deaf children to acquire language in the same way that hearing children do.

Being fluent in ASL is critical for deaf children's socialization and emotional well-being. When deaf children can communicate with their peers and adults in their community, they are more likely to develop strong social connections and feel a sense of belonging. This is why there are so many Deaf clubs and agencies. Community is important.

Academic success in deaf children is often predicated by ASL fluency. Children who are fluent in ASL tend to have better reading and writing skills in English than those who lack fluency. In addition, early exposure to communication and fluency in ASL also correlates to the deaf child having better memory skills and spatial reasoning abilities.

So, where do we go from here? We educate ourselves and others. Parents can still embrace the new technologies while encouraging fluency in ASL for themselves and their deaf children. One of the strongest places to learn sign language is through the nonprofit organization American Society for Deaf Children. They are the oldest national organization founded by and governed by parents with Deaf children. Check it out. Go to www.deafchildren.org today to learn more.

Mom Dad Not Hear

MOM HAS CANCER - DAD IS DEAD

"There are some phone calls you never forget.
They change your life in an instant,
shattering your world forever."
Jodi Picoult, author

Two phone calls

Like you, I've had countless phone calls that come in one ear and go out the other. A few of them I still remember, but two phone calls are permanently etched in my memory—I can recall every detail like they happened yesterday.

The first phone call...

I had graduated from college and was living in a house with three other guys whom I knew from college. My sister was away from home for her freshman year at Spring Arbor University. It was a Friday night; I had just wrapped up my work week. My cell phone rang, and I noticed it was my Grandma Jackson's number. This was unusual. Normally, she would never call me in the evening unless it was something that shouldn't wait—and typically that meant bad news.

"Mickey, your mother's biopsy came back today, and she has breast cancer." Grandma Jackson had taken to using "Deaf blunt" language—so no wasted words.

Ever since my mother had discovered a lump in her breast, we all knew this was possible. She had gone to the doctor the week before to discover the definitive truth about that lump, whether it was cancerous or nothing to worry about. The doctor sent a sample to the lab, and unfortunately, the test results came back positive. My mother had cancer.

I sat there in shock on the phone with my grandma, and my tears started to flow. Here I was away from home during a time when my mother needed me. I had very little experience with cancer, and in my mind, cancer meant imminent death. I was lost in my thoughts, dwelling on the worst possible outcomes, admitting my hopeless fear and heart-rending grief through my tears. My grandma tried to comfort me. She explained that it was fortunate that my mother had discovered the lump when she did. Because of that, the cancer had not spread beyond her breast, and she had decided to quickly proceed with the doctor's recommendation of a double mastectomy.

My mother valued health over vanity, and she wanted that cancer gone from her body. Her doctor told her that removing both breasts was the treatment with the highest success rate at this stage. The quicker my mother had the surgery, the sooner she could be cancer-free and on the road to recovery. So that's what she did.

And fortunately, the operation was a success, and my mother is still with us today. She's a cancer survivor. It's been two decades and counting, and we're thankful that cancer is behind her.

Now, the second phone call...

This one is a little more recent and even more impactful. I remember the date—April 30, 2021, shortly after 6 pm. Again, it was a Friday. My wife was still at work, and I was outside enjoying the Michigan spring weather with my children. My phone rang, and I looked down to see my Uncle Neil's name on the screen. It wasn't often that I got a call from him, so I answered quizzically and asked, "What's going on?"

"It's not good, Mickey. Your father passed away." He continued, "Your mother found him when she got home from work today." It was like someone had hit me with a baseball bat. I collapsed, falling to one knee—in total shock and disbelief. My son and daughter saw me and called out, asking what was wrong. We were in the neighbors' driveway, they heard the commotion and came out at just the right moment to take the kids into their house, realizing I needed some privacy.

I gathered myself the best I could and made three calls of my own: one to my wife, asking her to please come home right now, one to my sister arranging to meet her so we could go be with our mother, and finally, a call to my in-laws asking if they would come over to be with the kids until my wife, Erin, got home.

My entire life changed that day.

Later, I looked back at those two calls and realized that while they were both emotionally charged events that I couldn't have prepared for, at least I'm glad that in the heat of those moments, I didn't make any emotional or rash decisions.

You will get the calls eventually

Unfortunately, you will someday get calls like the two I just described—if you haven't received them already. It's the circle of life; we should expect it. But that doesn't make it any easier. As I think about those calls years later, they still haunt me, and I get emotional.

There are defining moments in our lives that reveal who we really are. How we react in those intense moments could determine the outcome of our next hours, days, and years as we continue forward. Whatever next steps you take after receiving a traumatic call starts with your initial reaction and first decision.

It's common for people to vividly remember significant and emotional events, especially traumatic ones. The phone calls I received informing me of my father's death and my mother's cancer diagnosis were extremely impactful and emotionally charged, and as a result, my brain encoded those memories more deeply than others. It happens to all of us because a part of the brain called the amygdala activates the release of stress hormones when we experience emotionally charged events, and that brain activity can enhance memory formation. This can lead to particularly vivid and long-lasting memories of traumatic events.

It's important to recognize that everyone processes and copes with trauma differently, and it's normal to experience a wide range of emotions and responses. If you find that certain memories are significantly impacting your day-to-day life or causing you distress, it may be helpful to seek support from a mental health professional.

We will inevitably all receive traumatic calls sooner or later. Start preparing for it. Beginning today, when you get any kind of bad news, don't let it rob you of your sense of reason. Don't react in a way that raises the emotion of the moment. Instead, take the time you need to absorb the news, determine what needs to be done, and put things in order so the outcome is something you can be proud of when you look back on that moment.

THE MEASURE OF
MY SUPERMAN

*"A father is a man who expects his son to be
as good a man as he meant to be."*
Frank A. Clark, lawyer and politician

The Eulogy

It's Wednesday, May 5, 2021, a day that has come much sooner than I ever thought it would. Fortunately, I'm surrounded by family and close friends—and I'm grateful as this is a day when someone in my shoes needs to know they are not alone.

I'm about to deliver the most difficult speech I've ever been asked to make...my father's eulogy. Mine is not the only speech; my sister and several other people share their memories of this man and the impact his life had on them. I half-listen as I shuffle through my note cards, one side of my brain focused on doing a great job to honor my father and the other side distracted by the fact that he is no longer with us. I realize that all the other speakers have finished, and the podium is empty. I stand and walk forward tentatively but resolutely. In my mind flashes an image of the changing of the guards at the

Tomb of the Unknown Soldier in Arlington National Cemetery. My walk becomes purposeful and solemn, like that of the honor guards. I am participating in a ceremonial passing of the guard. In my hand, I hold six notecards.

(Years later, as I sit at my home office desk, I glance away from my computer screen and see those same six notecards. I framed them and placed them prominently to remind me of that moment and my father.)

I place the cards on the podium, glancing at the first one. I look up to see the faces of people I've known all my life, and I begin to speak…

"This is the most difficult thing I have had to do in my life. Thank you to everyone who showed your respect for our father and our Superman—Sky Carolan.

To many, Superman is a fictional character—a protector of the world from evil. To me, Superman was real—he was my Dad.

For nearly 40 years I have been blessed to have a father that loved me. He was involved, present, and he truly cared about his family. My Superman gave me experiences and memories that a father should give his son.

Was our relationship perfect? No, it was real. There never was, and there never will be, a question of our love and respect for one another as father and son.

I have heard many stories over the past few days that bring me laughter and peace. Every story is a memory for me. I would like to take a moment to share some stories I recall.

Story one: The Sumo Wrestler Stomp

Dad bowled for a number of years, and his character and humor would come through on the lanes. He would often tuck his bowling towel into his pants and when he threw a strike, he would turn around and stomp like a sumo wrestler!

Story two: Homers vs. Singles

We had a mutual love early on. The ball diamond. I wanted to be my dad. I dressed like him and followed him everywhere I could. While our love was the same, our games could not have been more different.

He was a dead pull power hitter, and I was a contact hitter. I remember vividly his home run trophies. In my early 20s, I hit my first home run in fastpitch softball. He congratulated me and laughed at the same time. His response was: I hit more home runs in one inning than you have your entire career! He hit homers, and I hit singles.

The best part of our family's love for the game is that Dad and I weren't the best ball players in our family. Pound-for-pound, his daughter was, and he would tell everyone that fact with pride.

Speaking of pride—Story three: His grandchildren

He has four fantastic grandchildren. Olivia, Carson, Elloree, and Brooks. Dad has always been proud of his name; he taught Tammy and me to honor and protect our name. He cherished every moment he spent with *the next generation, and he was proud to see his name live on.*

Dad—your work here is done; we have your legacy from here. I love you."

Everyone deserves a Superman

Superman was my father's favorite superhero. And as I mentioned in this eulogy, my father was my Superman. I firmly believe everyone needs a Superman.

In my mind, Superman is strong, reliable, and always arrives when help is needed. Your Superman can help you face the many challenges and obstacles you encounter throughout your life. Having a Superman in your corner can make those challenges shrink before your very eyes, making them easier to conquer.

My Superman provided me with a constant sense of safety, security, and emotional support. Knowing he was there and that I could count on him boosted my confidence tremendously because I knew he loved me, believed in me, and supported me unconditionally.

I was fortunate to be blessed with a Superman. But I know that many are not. And if that happens to be you, I truly empathize. My Superman is gone, and I know how it feels. I'm sad for both of us.

Whether you have ever had a Superman or not in your life, here's what I want you to do today. If, like me, you know your Superman (or Superwoman), then carry that person's legacy with you and use it to give you strength, inspiration, and courage to stand up for what you believe in and defeat the obstacles that stand in your way. If you've never had a Superperson in your life, take positive steps today to break that cycle. Look for the person in your life who is there for you when you need them and look for ways to be strong for someone else who needs to know you're in their corner. I'll bet you're already someone's Superman—whether you know it or not.

THE STEALTH PHOTOGRAPHER

"Smile, you're on Candid Camera."
Allen Funt, creator and host of Candid Camera

Candid camera

"Look at this old shoe box full of videotapes," I signed as I pulled the box out of my old bedroom closet and handed it to my mother. As we looked through its contents, I saw more than twenty 8mm videotapes, some labeled with a description and some not. Some looked interesting, but hey, it was 2022, what was I supposed to do with one 8mm videotape, let alone a box of more than twenty of them? I didn't have any machine that could play them, and my mom didn't even know what was on them.

I was close to tossing them into the trash when a friend told me about a service that would transfer the tapes into digital video files. I picked out the tapes that were labeled and decided to give it a shot. When I received the digitized videos, I was amazed! This stuff was *gold*: shots of me playing in the three sports in which I competed as a child and footage of my graduations from high school and college.

I had no idea those videos existed. They had all been shot without my knowing that it was happening. That's only possible when you're the son of a stealth photographer.

As I thought back on my father's fondness for taking candid photos of his family, I remembered a photo that was displayed in our home as I was growing up. It was a surprise photo that my father took of my mother while they were on their honeymoon at the Grand Canyon. It was a great photo that captured a special moment. After that, he never stopped taking pictures and shooting candid videos. He was our family's Allen Funt (the original host of the long-running *Candid Camera* television program).

Science has discovered that when someone does not have use of one of their senses, the area of the brain that would be used to process the input from that sense (like hearing) doesn't remain unused. Instead, it gains function to augment another sense. Interestingly, research has shown that deafness correlates with an enhanced ability to perceive moving objects, increased peripheral vision capabilities in the retina itself, and increased visual attention.[9] So that might explain some of my father's passion and giftedness in photography.

My dad pursued this passion with quite an assortment of cameras. In addition to those 8mm tapes, I found all the old photography and video gear he had collected over the years, sitting in their cases, right next to the tapes.

My father's prime candid camera season was during his 35mm camera phase. That was a film camera, which meant that you couldn't see the photo right after taking it. Instead, when the roll of film was used up (24 or 36 shots later) it had to be taken to a darkroom service to be developed and printed. Once he got the packet of photographs home, he'd look them over with my mother. Invariably, she would give him an expression of annoyance and sign, "Why?" Sometimes, that look would also involve a light slap on his shoulder and a laugh.

Digital photography soon leveled the playing field for my mother, who was often the victim of his candid shots. As she became more accustomed to taking photos with her phone, our family text messages often included a photo she had taken of our father lounging in his chair, head back, mouth open, sawing logs. We laughed every single time she sent one!

Take the photo

As annoying as it might seem to be caught on Sky Carolan's candid camera, his love for taking photos and videos of our family's special moments and milestones was a blessing. He was not shy about being the father with a camera at a sporting event. He'd get as close as he could, recording the game, often holding the monstrosity of a video camera on his shoulder for hours.

He understood the importance of capturing those moments so that they could live on and be remembered and cherished later in life. Back then, it was a more difficult and expensive activity, but today it seems as if every moment, regardless of significance, is being captured on somebody's phone—and immediately posted to social media.

Photos and videos help us remember the details of events that might otherwise fade from our memories. Reviewing those details can bring back strong emotions and nostalgic feelings that we might otherwise have forgotten.

You never know what you'll find when you start digging through boxes of photos and memorabilia that have been collecting dust. But once you do, it's important to think about how to preserve what you uncover. Saving those images in a place where you can easily find them again is as important as taking the photo. Organize your photos and videos into folders on external hard drives or upload them to a cloud storage service. Either way, label them well so that the next generation won't need to wonder where to find them or accidentally discard the memories you've captured. Once you've decided how you will archive those images, keep them up to date by adding the most recent photos and files, so you can keep all your memories safe and accessible.

Family photos are some of our most cherished possessions. They capture happy memories and moments that we want to keep forever. So, starting today, whether you are sneaky like my father, or you're a more reserved photographer, the lesson is still the same: always take the photo or video. Future generations will thank you for it. Some great laughs, smiles, and tears can be shared over an old photo or video. So, start taking more family photos and videos today!

Mom Dad Not Hear

THEIR LEGACY LIVES ON

*"Please think about your legacy, because
you're writing it every day."*
Gary Vaynerchuk, author and entrepreneur

Love letter

I asked my daughter recently, "Do you know what a legacy is?" She looked at me quizzically and shrugged her shoulders. I said, "It's what I want to leave with you when I die—not just money to take care of you, but memories of all the things we've done together, places we've been, special events our family has celebrated, and the fun times we've had. I want to be sure you remember me and smile when you do." "Oh Dad," she said, rolling her eyes as she left the room to do something else.

Like many men and women, I find myself at times pondering my legacy. I wonder what people will remember about me when I die. Will I be thought of as outstanding, or just somewhat above average? What will I have accomplished that outlasts me? Will I have made an impact on anyone?

My parents pondered these questions as well. They didn't need to worry. I can tell you that my mother and father will be remembered for having made an impact. They influenced not just my life, but the lives of countless other people.

My mother and father had far different life stories than I did, and different than that experienced by most people. From the moment they took their first breath, their worlds were silent. They could see, smell, taste, and feel. But they could not hear.

From day one, they have been at a disadvantage, but they never felt like they were victims. They experienced the "otherness" of being Deaf, but they worked and fought to have equality. My mother and father did not give up. They believed that they could do the things that other people did—and that nothing should hold them back just because they were born Deaf.

I've often wondered how they processed the problems and challenges they encountered. How did they rise to overcome their obstacles, rather than falling prey to adversity? I know them better than most people do, yet this piece of their legacy, I still cannot comprehend.

My mother's story is one of compassion and love. Every day of her life, she had the comfort of knowing that she was supported and strengthened by a family that loved her unconditionally. Even as a young girl, her parents were making wise decisions to help prepare her to function in a hearing world.

The love, wisdom, and training that was poured into my mother took root deep within her, and from it, she grew into the woman that I have looked up to every day of my life. That strong foundation was vital because very few mothers have faced the pains that she has had to endure. First, there was me—a child with a physical disability that necessitated numerous trips to the hospital. Then, along came my sister, a premature baby whose home for the first three months of her tiny life was the hospital. One of my mother's deepest pains was the loss of my little brother Jay, who died before he even got to see the world and the family that already loved him so much. Those were just some of the challenges with her children.

Later, she battled breast cancer and fought it aggressively, undergoing life-altering and body-deforming surgeries—and she came out victorious. Then, after my father died far earlier than he should have, she had to learn how to live on her own.

Many women are given the privilege of living a calm, peaceful, "vanilla" kind of life. They grow up with all their senses, they have few complications with their children's births, and they are not diagnosed with cancer. Then there are others, like my mother, who've faced obstacles and hardships throughout their entire life but refuse to be defeated. Instead, for my mother, the trials that most people would see as major setbacks became the setup for her comeback. It's long been said, "What doesn't kill you makes you stronger,"[10] and that has proven true in my mother's life.

She not only inspired me and impacted my life, but Mom is one of the strongest women I have ever known. She has handled every painful thing life has thrown at her with grit and fierce determination. She demonstrated true love and compassion to my sister and me. She showed us what loyalty looks like—loyalty to my father, to her employer, and to her children. She displayed patience and tolerance. The ice in my veins today, and in my sister's, came directly from our mom. Someday my mother's life will end, but her memory will certainly live on. She will be remembered—and remembered well by many, including people who hope to be as tough as she proved to be. That will be my mother's legacy.

A Different Story

Now, my father's story was quite different. There is not a person that I have had a more volatile relationship with than my father—from our combative interactions in my late teen years to our shared tears of joy later in life.

My father, in stark contrast to my mother, did not grow up with a sense of security and stability. His life was marked by instability. Born to a father named Joseph and raised by a stepfather named Hank, my dad had more worries than most other young boys.

His adaptation to the world of hearing children was much more turbulent than my mom's. There was no decision made to send him to the Michigan School for the Deaf so he would be educated and cared for by people who were focused on providing an education with an ASL foundation. Instead, he was enrolled in the local public school where he was the only Deaf kid and felt like an outcast.

That was where his legacy began. My father faced the social stigma of exclusion very early in his life, and it became important to him to prove himself. He wanted to feel equal and be accepted. My father spent his entire childhood feeling different and ostracized, and in many respects, it was the same story during much of his adult life, as well. For every group or activity that he was interested in, he tried to prove he should be accepted into and included. If a conversation was happening anywhere near him, he wanted to know what was being said and have a voice in that discussion.

My memories of my father are grand. His athletic prowess during his younger years, his sense of humor, and his desire to be the center of attention. You always knew when my father was in the room. He was loud and vivacious, and he was also a man of extreme pride. He took pride in being the man of the house, and he made sure his family knew it. His unstable childhood and the lack of a strong fatherly influence made him desire to model the opposite for his family—by being a man who took care of his loved ones. I never doubted his love for my sister and me or his pride in each of our accomplishments.

I learned a lot from my father. Most of the sports that I've played were a direct result of learning from him. He took on a side job as an umpire, sacrificing his time at home, to be sure that our household had the economic stability to provide a great childhood for my sister and me. I used to think he just loved sports, and he did, but being an official was how he paid for us to have the opportunities we took for granted.

He also taught me how to be a leader. Many of the leadership skills I use today are a direct result of my father's influence and modeling. He showed me that in his isolated world, leaders must show conviction and stand true to what they feel is right. When people look back at my father's life, the legacy they see is that of a man who wanted to have an impact on the world. And he did.

Impact the world

To some people, legacy doesn't seem to be all that important. To others, like me, it's one thing that drives me daily. As entrepreneur Gary Vaynerchuk said, "Please think about your legacy, because you're writing it every day." For many people, understanding the importance of leaving a legacy doesn't click until much later in life, when it's often too late. For me, it took reaching the milestone of being forty years old and losing my father, to understand that I still have the opportunity to do something more with my life...and the opportunity to leave more.

Every year I choose one word to be my theme for the year, an idea I got from best-selling author Jon Gordon. In 2022, my word was "Legacy." In 2023, my word is "Finish." The kind of legacy I want to leave—success that impacts generations to come—was initiated by the legacy of two Deaf parents who defied the odds. My word for 2023 has strategic implications as well. I've always been a great "starter" but a mediocre "finisher." Writing, completing, and publishing this book was the number one goal I had in mind when I chose my word for the year.

Today, start thinking about how you want to be remembered. Consider what others might say about you at your funeral. Dream about the stories your grandchild will tell their kids about you and your life. Now, determine what you need to put in place to be the kind of person you want to become. Every year, perhaps at the New Year or on your birthday, or some other occasion you will always remember, evaluate how you are doing in the legacy department, and adjust as needed.

Understanding the importance of the legacy you will leave should influence you to make decisions with the end in mind. What you and I choose to do today is an opportunity to leave a legacy that can impact multiple generations in the future.

A CONVERSATION WITH MY MOTHER

"My mother was the making of me. She was so true, so sure of me; and I felt I had something to live for, someone I must not disappoint."
Thomas Edison, inventor and businessman

Mom, what were the challenges for you, growing up as a Deaf child in a hearing family?

Well, it was hard to communicate with my family. It was difficult communicating in sign language with my brothers, especially because I was only home on weekends. They couldn't practice ASL consistently. When I was at the Michigan School for the Deaf (MSD), my every conversation was in ASL. But when I came home, I walked into a hearing world where a different language was used. Communication was the biggest challenge.

When you married Dad, were you nervous about having children...with no idea if they would be Deaf or able to hear?

We were a little bit afraid of having children. Before you and your sister were born, we *did* wonder if we would have Deaf or hearing children. Even though you were born with the ability to hear, your father and I made it a point to teach you American Sign Language. We also knew that we needed to involve you in the hearing world, which we did by encouraging you to take part in extracurricular activities with other hearing children. We had you try as many sports and activities as you wanted to help you form relationships with your peers.

How did you first know that I could hear as a baby, and what were your feelings and fears then?

The nurses confirmed that you passed your hearing test while we were still in the hospital. We were nervous, in general, because we were first-time parents. Our larger concern was your cleft lip and cleft palate. At that point, we already knew we'd teach you ASL as your first language since we were told you would develop speech more slowly than most other children.

What do you think you and Dad did well in raising two hearing children?

While we didn't have much money, we tried our best to make sure you didn't want for much. That was part of the reason your father started um-piring. He used the extra money to pay for the various activities that you and your sister participated in. We also showed you the importance of hard work and grit in our daily lives. You were able to see some of the challenges we faced.

What were the most difficult challenges for you?

Communication with people outside of my native language of ASL has been the greatest challenge.

Was I a difficult child to raise? Tell me some examples or stories you remember.

No, you and your sister were good kids. The biggest trouble we had with you was during your teenage years. You were trying to grow up, which meant increased independence, and you would get frustrated when we would put demands on your time to interpret for us. The main issue we had was when you wanted to play with your friends, and we interrupted your fun time because we needed your help to make a phone call or to help us communicate with someone who didn't know ASL.

What advice would you give Deaf parents of hearing children?

Support your children and get them involved in many social environments to broaden their exposure to the hearing world. Don't take their interpreting for granted and use their help only when it is needed—allow them to still be children.

What advice would you give hearing parents who are raising a Deaf child?

Well, I am a little old-school. I believe if you are born Deaf, you should learn ASL and embrace your deafness. I did not have the technology that is available today, but being able to fluently communicate in ASL is important. I want parents to know that they will have tough decisions to make sometimes. The communication challenges I have had are real, but they can also be difficult if you try to force a Deaf child away from ASL. There are plenty of horror stories of parents who did not embrace a balanced approach to communication. So, make wise use of technology, but also don't neglect what has worked well in the Deaf community.

What do you wish that hearing people understood about being Deaf?

That we can do anything other people can do, except hear things.

What else would you like to add that we haven't talked about?

The fact that you're writing stories now as an adult doesn't surprise me. When you were in elementary school you entered a story contest and won a t-shirt for your work. And now, here you are telling our family stories through the written word, many years later!

LESSONS FROM PART THREE
LOVE

1 **Communicate so your message is easily understood to show that you care.** Even a basic attempt at using a person's native language will be appreciated. When you encounter someone who has English as their second language, make an effort to meet them in their world. Focus on the person you're talking to—and try speaking to their heart and not just their head.

2 **Find a community that loves you and one that you can love back!** Investing your time as part of a supportive community will enable you to better cope with difficult challenges, find help in solving problems, and celebrate life's successes. Find a community that truly cares about its members and give them more than you receive.

3 **Be an advocate—stand up for yourself.** Advocate for the people you love and care about. And don't neglect those who are powerless to speak for themselves. You can speak up for them; they need your help. Excel at expressing empathy.

4 **Overcome communication barriers with those around you by seeking solutions to remove the obstacle.** Keep an open mind, and whether it's a new technology that provides the key, or spending the time that interpersonal communication requires, embrace the solution, and celebrate the breakthroughs. Anything that improves the quality of your communication with family and friends is worth it.

5 **Parents should do everything they can to ensure that their children grow up being fluent in their heart language.** For Deaf children that is American Sign Language. By gaining fluency they will see gains in communication skills and language development, socialization, academic success, and cognitive development.

6 **There are defining moments in our lives that reveal who we really are.** You will inevitably receive traumatic news sooner or later. Start preparing for it now, and when you get bad news, don't react with a knee-jerk emotion. Instead, absorb the news, determine what needs to be done, and take action so the outcome is something you can be proud of.

7 **Look for a person in your life who is there when you need them and show them how much you value them.** Also, look for ways to be strong for someone else who needs to know you're in their corner. Find your Superman and be someone's Superman!

8 **Take more photos—some will turn out to be priceless, cherished memories of important moments.** Save those images in a place where you can easily find them again. Organize your photos and videos and label them so that the next generation won't wonder what they are or where to locate them.

9 **Impact your world!** Understand the importance of leaving a legacy of how you want to be remembered. Consider what others might say about you at your funeral. Dream about the stories your grandchild will tell their kids about you and your life. Determine what kind of person you want to become and take steps now to make that vision a reality.

10 **Have quality conversations with the people who have impacted you in your life.** It could be parents—birth, adoptive, or adults who filled that role. It might be teachers or other leaders who helped you become the person you are today. Track them down and take the time to have a heartfelt conversation with them. Record it so you can relive it at a later date. Thank them for the impact they had on your life and tell them you love them.

ACKNOWLEDGMENTS

A sincere thank you for dedicating your valuable time to explore the pages of this book. Time stands as our most valuable asset, and your decision to allocate some of it to read these pages is deeply appreciated. Your readership serves as the driving force propelling this book on its journey into the world.

To my parents, who gave me the gift of family and the opportunity to be a CODA. To Erin, my incredible wife, and our wonderful children, for creating our cherished family.

Bonnie Carolan, your hand served as the muse for Diana Lopez's brilliant cover artwork. Miblart team, your design work brought this book to life.

To Joe and Kathy Sindorf, thank you for partnering with me in crafting the magic within these pages. Phil deHaan, your eagle-eyed editing shaped this manuscript with precision.

Aryn Van Dyke, the Book Rockstar, your guidance justifies why you are one of the best in the business.

To Tammy Kolenda, Deb Atwood, and Marc Carolan, your meticulous review ensured factual accuracy.

Lane Walker, my friend and mentor, your invaluable guidance is deeply appreciated.

Sara Novic, your willingness to engage and answer my questions was immeasurable help.

To Jon Acuff, thank you for writing your book, Finish. It was my one word for 2023 and served as a reminder to FINISH this book.

To Jamie Lemmen, Mary Fenech, Jennifer Salgat, Kate Van Auken, and Patrick Swain, thank you for your pivotal feedback and encouragement.

To Ben Newman, Alexis Ander Kashar, Kim Dabbs, Sue Schmidlkofer, Bill McKendry, Brad Klein, Keith Wann, and Cheri Dowling, your endorsements illuminate the reasons behind this book.

A tip of the hat to the Tri-City Association of the Deaf, where I learned the true meaning of community.

To the board, staff, and community at Deaf and Hard of Hearing Services, thank you for being my connectivity to the Deaf community in West Michigan.

To friends and family who learned ASL to communicate with my parents, your efforts did not go unnoticed, bridging the language gap.

To the Akron-Fairgrove farm community, thank you for embracing our family and nurturing an environment where leadership could flourish.

To UPS, thank you for providing a career where I apply these lessons daily.

To all support organizations mentioned ahead, keep doing great work; the community needs your continued energy.

Lastly, Erin, there are not enough ways to express my gratitude. Your care and insightful feedback make me a better husband, father, and man every day. You were the first to read this story and offer feedback, the cornerstone of both me and this incredible journey together.

SUPPORT RESOURCES

Agencies I have personally worked with:

Deaf and Hard of Hearing Services (DHHS): DHHS is a community-based organization in West Michigan established in 1995. DHHS provides a range of services, including sign language interpreting, advocacy, education, and support for deaf and hard-of-hearing individuals. Website: https://deafhhs.org/

American Society for Deaf Children (ASDC): The American Society for Deaf Children (ASDC) is a non-profit organization dedicated to supporting and advocating for deaf and hard-of-hearing children and their families. Founded in 1967, ASDC provides a range of resources, information, and networking opportunities to empower families and promote the optimal development of deaf and hard-of-hearing children. Website: https://deafchildren.org

Deaf Community Advocacy Network – DEAF C.A.N.! - Deaf Community Advocacy Network – DEAF C.A.N.! is a non-profit Organization established in 1981 to provide services to the thousands of Deaf and Hard of Hearing people living in southeastern

Michigan. DEAF C.A.N.! offers direct client services to individuals and families, as well as community education and information for professional groups. Website: https://deafcan.org

CODA International: CODA International, short for "Children of Deaf Adults" International, is an organization that serves individuals who are hearing and have deaf parents or other family members. CODA International recognizes and supports the unique experiences and perspectives of CODAs, individuals who grow up in homes where American Sign Language (ASL) is commonly used, and deaf culture is an integral part of their lives. Website: https://www.coda-international.org/

But wait there's more!

National Level Resources:

National Association of the Deaf (NAD): The NAD is the oldest and largest civil rights organization for the deaf and hard-of-hearing community in the U.S. They provide advocacy, information, and resources on various issues related to deafness. Website: https://www.nad.org/

Registry of Interpreters for the Deaf (RID): RID offers information and support for sign language interpreters, as well as resources for deaf individuals seeking interpreters for various settings. Website: https://www.rid.org/

National Deaf Center on Postsecondary Outcomes (NDC): NDC provides resources and support to deaf individuals pursuing higher education and successful transitions to the workforce. Website: https://www.nationaldeafcenter.org/

Deaf Women United (DWU): DWU focuses on the empowerment of deaf women through education, advocacy, and networking. Website: https://dwu.org/

Gallaudet University: Gallaudet is a renowned university for deaf and hard of hearing students. Their website offers various resources, including information on deaf culture, American Sign Language (ASL) resources, and research. Website: https://www.gallaudet.edu/

Hands & Voices: Hands & Voices is a non-profit organization that supports families and their children who are deaf or hard of hearing, regardless of communication mode or educational approach. Website: https://handsandvoices.org/

Laurent Clerc National Deaf Education Center: The Laurent Clerc National Deaf Education Center is a federally funded organization that focuses on improving the quality of education for deaf and hard of hearing students from birth through age 21. The center is named after Laurent Clerc, a renowned educator who played a crucial role in establishing the first permanent school for the deaf in the United States, the American School for the Deaf. Website: https://gallaudet.edu/clerc-center/

UNLOCKING CONVERSATIONS - A BOOK CLUB DISCUSSION GUIDE

Deaf Culture and Identity:

- How does the book shed light on the experiences and challenges faced by the CODA community?
- How does the author navigate his dual cultural identity as both a hearing individual and a member of the Deaf community?
- In what ways does the memoir illustrate the importance of preserving and celebrating Deaf culture?

Family Dynamics and Communication:

- How does having Deaf parents impact the author's family dynamics and communication methods?
- How does the memoir highlight the different modes of communication used by the author's family, and what do these choices signify?
- What insights does the book provide into the role of communication and understanding within diverse families?

Diversity, Equity, and Inclusion:

- How does the author's journey reflect the broader themes of diversity, equity, and inclusion?
- In what ways does the memoir challenge common misconceptions or stereotypes about the Deaf community?
- How do the author's experiences contribute to conversations about creating inclusive spaces for individuals from diverse backgrounds?

Accessibility and Advocacy:

- What barriers to accessibility and inclusion does the author encounter in his journey, and how do they address them?
- How does the memoir illustrate the importance of advocating for accessibility and equal opportunities for all?
- What lessons can readers take away from the author's advocacy efforts in promoting accessibility?

Intersectionality and Empathy:

- How does the author's story intersect with other dimensions of his identity, such as ethnicity, gender, or socio-economic background?
- How does the memoir prompt readers to develop empathy and understanding for individuals who navigate multiple aspects of their identity?

- How can readers apply the lessons of empathy and intersectionality to their own lives and interactions?

Educational and Societal Impact:

- How does the memoir shed light on the challenges and opportunities that Deaf individuals encounter within educational and societal contexts?
- How does the author's experiences inform discussions about educational systems, accommodations, and the role of awareness in fostering change?
- What changes or improvements could be made to educational systems and society to better support Deaf individuals and other marginalized communities?

Personal Growth and Resilience:

- How does the author's personal growth and resilience throughout their journey inspire readers to overcome challenges and embrace change?
- What moments in the memoir illustrate the author's ability to adapt, learn, and grow from their experiences?
- How can readers apply the lessons of resilience and growth to their own lives?

AUTHOR BIO

Mickey Carolan

Author Mickey Carolan is a storyteller with a unique perspective. Growing up with two Deaf parents, he became fluent in one of the most beautiful languages in the world, American Sign Language. Fueled by a passion to honor his family's remarkable legacy, Mickey's words leap off the page, inviting readers into his world.

Nestled just outside the vibrant hub of Grand Rapids, Michigan, Mickey shares his life with his cherished wife, Erin, and their dynamic duo, Elloree, and Brooks. Amidst the hustle and bustle of optimizing global supply chains and being his wife's trusty cheerleader in the salon realm, Mickey finds inspiration in writing about leadership and the intricate dance of life.

Beyond the keyboard, Mickey finds joy in a variety of roles – a family man devoted to his loved ones, a youth sports coach molding future champions, an avid reader delving into diverse realms of thought, and a fitness enthusiast who finds strength not only in lifting weights but in the weights of life's experiences.

Mickey Carolan adds a new layer to the legacy he seeks to preserve with every word he crafts. Through his stories, we're reminded that the beauty of life lies not just in its smooth paths, but in the unexpected twists and turns that shape us.

Join Mickey on social media for more adventures and community.

LinkedIn: www.linkedin.com/in/mickeycarolan
Facebook: Mickey Carolan – Author & Speaker
Instagram: @CarolanOnMyMind

Book Mickey for a Live or Virtual Event!

Website: www.MickeyCarolan.com

JOSEPH & KATHLEEN SINDORF

Kathleen and Joseph Sindorf are award-winning communicators who love to help people touch hearts with clarity and impact. As a tenured university professor and veteran international filmmaker, this duo loves stories and telling stories well. Learn more about them at wordsmiths.pro.

ALSO BY

Children's Books:

Sky, the Deaf Home Run Hero: A Lesson in Courage (Deaf Kids Can #1)

Bonnie and the Deaf Bake Squad: A Lesson in Confidence (Deaf Kids Can #2)

ENDNOTE SECTION

1 - "About Us," Deaf and Hard of Hearing Services, deafhhs.org, accessed April 17, 2023.

2 - "Nike 'Failure' Michael Jordan Ad 1997," https://www.youtube.com/watch?v=nvrbQBI4ElI, accessed May 9. 2023.

3 - "Deaf People and Economic Well-Being: A Research Summary," by Barbara Gerner de Garcia and Rosalinda B. Barrera, Queen's University Belfast, https://pureadmin.qub.ac.uk/ws/portalfiles/portal/139858103/Kim_Byrne_and_Parish_LOS_final_manu_revised3PURE.pdf, accessed June 21, 2023.

4 - "How a Second Language Can Boost the Brain" by Ramin Skibba, Knowable Magazine, https://knowablemagazine.org/article/mind/2018/how-second-language-can-boost-brain?gclid=Cj0KCQjwtsCgBhDEARIsAE7RYh0h7-6ZaXn9-K70Mc5tG43TUb0Ofiy_vY_g6E0LtnfTe1WSK_LhJfAaAlj8EALw_wcB, accessed June 21, 2023.

5 - Ibid.

6 - A name sign is a sign that is exclusively given to one person, and it is usually created based on the person's characteristics, personality, hobbies, etc, which uniquely and distinctively identify a person, "Deaf Culture/Name Signs," Start ASL, https://www.startasl.com/name-signs/, accessed May 15, 2023.

7 - "Why Deaf Children Need ASL, American Society for Deaf Children, https://deafchildren.org/2019/02/why-deaf-children-need-asl/, accessed April 23, 2023.

8 - "Position Statement on Early Cognitive and Language Development and Education of Deaf and Hard of Hearing Children," National Association of the Deaf, https://www.nad.org/about-us/position-statements/position-statement-on-early-cognitive-and-language-development-and-education-of-deaf-and-hard-of-hearing-children/, accessed April 23, 2023.

9 - "Do Hearing Impaired People Use Other Senses Better?"Audicus, https://www.audicus.com/do-hearing-impaired-people-use-other-senses-better/, accessed June 21. 2023.

10 - "Science Proves That What Doesn't Kill You Makes You Stronger," Northwestern Now, https://news.northwestern.edu/stories/2019/10/science-proves-that-what-doesnt-kill-you-makes-you-stronger/, accessed May 16, 2023.

Mom Dad Not Hear

www.ingramcontent.com/pod-product-compliance
Lightning Source LLC
Chambersburg PA
CBHW020450130626
46549CB00001B/363